BENEATH THE SURF

Beneath The Surface

LEARN FROM YOUR PAST, LIVE IN THE PRESENT, MANIFEST YOUR FUTURE.™

BY ZANE KEKOA SCHWEITZER

Zaniac Press 2017

Beneath The Surface

First Edition: Printed in the United States on FSC (Forest Stewardship Council) and SFI (Sustainable Forestry Initiative)

Eco-friendly paper and vegetable based ink

Cover Painting: Judie Vivian
Back cover image: © Kameron Pollock
Interior photos of Journal Pages: Judy Shasek
Art direction: Anne Marie Daggett, The Marketing Department
Cover and book design: Lieve Maas, BrightLightGraphics.com

ISBN: 978-1-5323-5974-3 (digital edition)
ISBN: 978-1-5323-5528-8 (print edition)

What lies "Beneath the Surface" of Zane Kekoa Schweitzer?

Svein Rasmussen, Founder and Chief of Starboard:
Zane Kekoa Schweitzer lives an absolutely inspiring life story. That story is just starting to unravel through this book, which is sort of the first chapter. He can help create a better world through his curiosity, willingness to learn and ability to energetically share very important lessons. Zane is taking the lead in so many aspects and to work with him on anything is a lot of fun.

Dave Kalama, Legendary Waterman:
Zane has a natural inclination to share his knowledge. He comes from a great family that has been instrumental in inspiring him to be the really good person he is. That is one of the key defining characteristics he has to his core. Zane possesses a lot of traditional waterman skills. The face and definition of the classic way of being a waterman is changing and Zane is the epitome of that evolution.

Michael Stewart, Founder of Sustainable Surf:
There is no doubt in my mind that Zane Schweitzer was born to be a world class Waterman. But more importantly, he's a natural born storyteller with something worth sharing – let's call it an "Attitude of Gratitude." That attitude along with his many globetrotting competitive successes as a professional ocean athlete, his natural curiosity

and respect about the world around him are what really make him a "world champion" worth "talking story" with. So, go ahead. Spend some time hanging out with Zane in his first book and you'll feel the way I always do after a conversation with him: inspired, refreshed, and stoked about the path ahead.

Cyrill Gutsch, Founder of Parley for the Oceans:
Zane is an innocent influencer, an energy infusion for our movement, an ocean warrior. He doesn't know the ideas of fear and doubt. His path is an inspiration for anyone wanting to dedicate his life to purpose.

Connor Baxter, Multi World Champion Waterman, Fastest Paddler on Earth:
Zane Kekoa Schweitzer has the biggest heart of anyone I know and can make anyone feel the "aloha spirit" of Hawai'i no matter where in the world he is. He is also one of the most talented watermen I have ever known.

Sage and grandma Carolyn locking eyes through four generations.
Photo Credit: Matty Schweitzer

Dedication

Dedication to my Grandma Carolyn Jackson

My grandmother Carolyn instilled life values in me at a young age. For that I will be forever grateful. Grandma Carolyn was always peaceful, always in a state of contentment and she was always there for the people around her. This included each one of my family members as well as so many others in my community. She was a counselor, therapist and angel to so many people young and old. Many were friends of my brother and myself. She worked for the public schools as a counselor to the most troubled kids and was a mother figure many never had. Most of the time she would keep food in her office, knowing how often students would show up to school with an empty stomach. She always had a way of instilling hope. Often, she would remind me, "Hope is what keeps faith alive, so keep hoping."

I remember walking through the park or the grocery store with my little old grandma. The most gnarly looking people would stop and open their heart to her. You could feel their love and gratitude for the support and hope she shared with them. My grandma was always my hero for that, not just for the hope, love and life lessons she instilled in me, but also because she shared with everyone around her. When we'd go shopping, she'd hardly look at what she picked out. She'd simply hold her hand over the food she passed and allowed her subconscious to pick out what she needed. She was more intellectually and spiritually connected than anyone I ever knew.

No matter what the problem or who was suffering, she would always know what to say. She maintained this connection with people even when she was in her last months of life. She would always know what to say. It was almost as though she could speak with a person's spirit. Grandma Carolyn taught me to respect God. She'd read me scriptures from books of Tao, books from the Dalai Lama and the Bible.

Ever since I could remember she nicknamed me, "Mister Enthusiasm," and always advocated this trait of mine. If I ever needed a place of peace or a place to escape, I'd go to my grandma's house. Her house was always organized, clean and had peace in the air. If I were on the road, I'd call her from afar and she'd comfort me with her words of wisdom. She had gifted her grandkids, including myself, with "gratitude beads." She made these from a variety of stones and crystals of different colors that we chose. There were seven large stones or crystals symbolizing the seven chakras. She'd assure us, "Gratitude is the root of happiness and there is always something to be grateful for, therefore you'll always be happy."

She would ask us to hold our gratitude beads and say something we are grateful for with every one of the large stones on the piece. She'd let us practice this even further by asking us to always recite something new and avoid saying the same thing twice. This practice taught me all the many ways we can embed gratitude in every day. I'll miss her and think about her every day when I practice my daily gratitude.

My grandmother always encouraged me to compile my journal entries and publish a book. She said I had a story worth telling. What she might not have realized was how much of my story, that I carry with me always, is built upon the lessons she taught me along the way. I hadn't completed this book before she passed away, but I know she was proud that I had taken her encouragement and that *Beneath the Surface* was going to be a reality.

This book is dedicated to my Grandmother Carolyn with love, and of course, an "attitude of gratitude."

"WALKING WITH CAROLYN"

From *Clarity with Carolyn* by Carolyn Jackson.

Come for a walk with me as I envelop myself in the abundance of Maui. Take a deep breath and see yourself cavorting with nature. This is the most wonderful way to start my day.

As I walked this morning it was not with a jogger's walk or an energetic stride, it was the walk of a child. I looked at everything around me; every bush and flower. I looked at all the people swimming, surfing, lounging, and dancing with the waves. As I watched all those people playing a smile took over my face. I was with each of these anonymous friends in spirit. They were having fun and I was a silent collaborator and those in front of me did not know at that moment in time I was playing with them in spirit. Just imagine a light breeze on your face, your hair blowing gracefully with the sound of the ocean as your music. Now you are with me.

The song in my mind is "make your own kind of music" and it encourages me to sway a little. It would be great to have an umbrella like Mary Poppins and sing loudly while I skip. Can you imagine what a memorable sight that would be? What a wonderful out of the norm childlike experience. What a liberating out of the box expression of joy!

How many of us are that capable of being true to our own inspiration? Should I do it? Should I get dressed and dance on the boardwalk? Should I completely embarrass my family? Mmmm, I think I should. What do you think?

When I am taking my walk I never allow a negative thought to enter my mind. My focus is on my breath, on the sights and sounds around me. I create a mantra of healing statements for the health of my mind and body. Nothing else enters. This was my experience on the boardwalk today. It was a good day.

Dedication to my Grandparents Diane and Hoyle Schweitzer

How proud I am to be a Schweitzer. My grandparents on my father's side are proof that dreams can be accomplished through following your heart and sharing with others. My grandmother Diane was the person who instilled the practice of journaling on me. She and her husband, my grandpa Hoyle, traveled the world for adventures they were passionate about. These adventures included; boating, sailing, surfing and bringing windsurfing to the world.

Both of my grandparents taught me to respect Mother Nature and not to be afraid of immersing myself in the world and its people. They proved to me, with all their stories of adventures and following their heart, that passion for life is powerful and can create freedom. When I first started following in their footsteps by traveling the world while practicing windsurfing, I found myself being open to opportunities that would come to me and adventures that would excite me. My grandma Diane gifted me my first journal at the time when I was beginning to be an adventurer myself. It was titled, *Devotion*.

She gave it to me at the beginning of my professional windsurfing career at the age of 12, telling me that one day I'd have many stories and adventures of my own to share with my family and friends. When presenting the journal to me she said, "It's important to share your experiences with the world and its people into your journal. It's not just for sharing with your family, but it's meant to be for yourself to remember those moments."

She'd tell me that one day I'll be old like her and Grandpa and may have a hard time remembering these moments. Grandma Diane shared, "If you write them down they'll never be forgotten."

The combination of the lessons my grandparents instilled in me were instrumental in my becoming an adventurous, passionate person myself and gave me the structure to develop my own philosophy for life.

Top: Pictured here is my 'ohana – my Grandfather Hoyle, and Grandmother Diane, my Dad Matt, my sister Shelby holding her dog Bella, my mom Shawneen, my Grandmother Carolyn, my brother Matty, his wife Elena, her mother Deanne, and me and my dog Kava.
Photo Credit: Schweitzer 'Ohana

Bottom: My Grandfather Hoyle, and Grandmother Diane
Photo Credit: Matty Schweitzer

Acknowledgments

This book could not have been brought to life without help and inspiration from so many. I am truly filled with gratitude.

To Grandma Carolyn - Thank you for teaching me to lead a life filled with an attitude of gratitude and for inspiring me to write this book. You are my angel.

To Grandma Diane and Grandpa Hoyle - I will always be grateful for you gifting me my first journal and enlightening me to see this world with an open mind and heart. "Wherever you go, go with all your heart."

To Mom - I feel so fortunate to have you always being there for me with love and support, and for always pushing me and giving me the confidence to know that I can do anything I set my mind to.

To Dad - I am lucky that you have shared your passion for life and nature, encouraged me to make every moment count, and demonstrated the lesson of humility with me by being the humble athlete, man, father, and husband you are.

To my brother Matty - thank you for being my best friend, big brother, coach, photographer/videographer, and travel partner. We have had some amazing times! Thank you for including me in your life as your five-year younger brother. I've been motivated and inspired by you (and your friends) for as long as I can remember and I'm proud to be your little brother. I'm also grateful for the times you've kept me in check – I wouldn't be who I am today without you.

To Shelby - My beautiful sister Shelby has opened up my eyes to the importance of leading my life with gentle kindness and to have compassion for all people and living things around me. You remind me of the satisfaction of being a Soul Surfer and to always keep in mind what may lie beneath their surface of others.

Top: My sister, Shelby, and I all smiles after surfing at Honolua Bay!
Photo Credit: Matty Schweitzer

Bottom: Matty and I throwing Shakas while exploring waterfalls in Tahiti.
Photo Credit: Georgia Schofield for the Schweitzer Ohana

To Judy Shasek - I am so honored to have been able to work with and learn from you. I can't thank you enough for your mentorship and guidance throughout this project. You were a huge motivation, inspiration and key influence for me. Without your guidance in putting my stories and experiences together into a book, they would have remained as just treasured journal entries. You spent as many hours as I did on this project, working from the love and aloha you have within. You believed that readers should see my world and its people through my experiences and memoirs. I am so grateful for your encouragement, your interest in my philosophy and your willingness to support what motivates me beneath my surface and what keeps me grounded. I hope this book makes you proud.

To Judie Vivian - Mahalo for donating your time and wonderful talent to create the artwork and cover of *Beneath the Surface*. Without any real direction from me, you created the amazing painting that resonated in your imagination after reading the first drafts of *Beneath the Surface*. I will cherish this and all the incredible paintings you have created for me and my family over the years. Mahalo for your aloha, love and support!

To all my sponsors and supporters - Mahalo for giving me the opportunity to create my own wave of success through your support of my goals and endeavors as a competitor and Environmental Aloha Ambassador. I wouldn't have been able to experience the world and its people or to be in the position I am without more than a decade of support from Starboard. I'm proud that I can believe in and trust in my supporters through both their mindsets and mission statements. Thank you, Maui Jim Sunglasses for allowing me to see the world with all its color. Mahalo to Cobian Footwear for the long-time support and a few of the best trips I have ever had. Your sandals keep me comfortable, grounded and remind me that "Every Step Matters." Honolua Surf Company sponsors not only me, but also my InZane SUPer Grom Clinics. That support has made a huge difference to the kids of Maui. Chris of Black Project Fins, I feel so fortunate for the opportunity to work with you. The support you give to me and to the InZane SUPer Groms is so appreciated. Mahalo, to Tom Abbott of the Palladium Hotel Group for believing in Team Hawaii and supporting our ISA events. Your hotels are amazing and I look forward to many more projects all over the world.

Mahalo to all the world class photographers for your donations and contributions to this book and quality captures of priceless moments; Matty Schweitzer / Mat5o Media, Erik Aeder, Damian / Dooma Photos, Brent Schlea, Kamryn Pollock, Mike Killion, Mike Neal, Sean Evans, Brian Bielman, Georgia Shofield, Harry Weiwel, and Abraham Shouse. It's a gift to get to work with such a talented and amazing group of photographers who capture the images that allow me to share my life with the world.

To my friends who remind me to remember where I came from and to make the most of every moment of my experiences with the world and its people. It means so much to share the experience with them through story as well.

To all the World Class Athletes I travel with all over the world - I feel stoked to have been able to create these memories with you, literally riding the best waves on the planet together. I couldn't mention every one of you in the book, but if you had read all of my journals I'm sure there are some great stories of each of you.

To my 'ohana and extended 'ohana; The Schweitzers, The Clawsons, The Pitzers, The Schleas, The Grants, the Larsens, The Kalamas, The Lickles, The Waltzes, Archie Kalepa, and my Kahana Nui 'Ohana. I may travel the world, but you all are always there with me in spirit. And to the Baxters, you are like family and I feel so honored that I have traveled with Connor for most of my adventures. Keith and Karen you were so fun to travel with as chaperones when we were young, you never stopped us from trying anything and that is probably why we are the athletes we are today!

To all the water safety teams that have been there to keep an eye on my brother and me, and to other surfers, so we could continue pushing the limits by doing what we love with confidence and to have longevity in this passion; Skullbase Team including the Walsh Ohana, Kolomona, Hawaiian Water Patrol, Victor Lopez, Archie Kalepa, Derek

Doerner, Milton Martinson, Uncle Mark, Kurtis Chong Kee, Nano, and the life guard crew from Flemings; including Freddy Vermey and the late Uncle Al.

Mahalo to all the event organizers and people in our industry that provide us athletes with the platform from which to perform and launch. For example, Tristan Boxford of the Waterman League who had faith enough in our sport to dedicate over a decade and his life to create the Standup World Tour and Standup World Series. These two tours are the source of most of my stories over the last decade. Mahalo, Fernando Aguerre, President of ISA, Chris Parker of SupRacer, Barrett Tester and countless more contest organizers that work tirelessly to promote our sports and share them with the masses. Greg Townsend, you have allowed me the opportunity to see the world beyond my imagination, while showcasing my pursuit of passion and dreams to become world champion in an incredible multi-discipline event like the Ultimate Waterman. Mahalo to my childhood mentors like Rodney Kilborn of Handsome Buggah Productions, Aunty Bobbi Lee of NSSA Hawaii, and Papa John and Aunty Donna Willard of Hawaii Surf Association, for giving so much time to the youth of Hawaii and starting us all so young. They have contributed greatly to surfing by producing some of the world's very best hailing from Hawai i. And how can I thank the magazines that have supported me and this sport; *Standup Journal*, *Sup the Mag*, *Standup Magazine*, *Sup International*, *Get Up*, *SUP Magazine*. The stories and images you share with the world have made our sport the fastest growing sport. Thank you!

To Sustainable Surf and Parley - Thank you for taking the time and for teaching me ways to use the platform I'm building not only for the benefit of myself, but for the benefit of my loved ones and our environment around us. The simple changes we make can change the world. And a big Mahalo to Hoku Haiku for his mana'o and teaching during the filming our documentary *Deep Blue Life*.

To Maui - Mahalo to the island and environment itself for shaping me into who I am today. Mahalo to my community for sharing your mana and aloha with me from day one and for inspiring me with the magic that Maui instills in people.

And to the countless unnamed people all over the world, that have supported and believed in me, I can't thank you enough. You continue to encourage me to *Innovate and Inspire* and *Believe and Create* every day!

Table of Contents

Foreword

Judy Shasek, Water Words: Zane and I were probably two of the least likely people to meet. It is Zane's consistent way of saying "yes" to ideas, opportunities and people that brought us together in late 2015. After reading his powerful social media posts from the 2016 Ultimate Waterman event in New Zealand and his experience with the Maori elders, I dug a bit deeper. I was curious to know, "who is Zane Kekoa Schweitzer?" I was familiar with Zane as the elite windsurfer, surfer, paddler, and waterman. But who was the philosophical guy with a strong practice of meditation and the philosophy to "Innovate and Inspire?"

We met over a two-hour breakfast in Lahaina, Maui. That get-together was non-stop stoke and stories from Zane. He listened with the same energy he put into sharing a story - full on engagement. As we said our goodbyes, as an aside, Zane mentioned that one day he would like to write a book based on his lifetime of journaling. Just as casually, I said I'd love to help in any way I could.

Fast forward to December 2016. My husband and I were back on Maui. Zane was committed to write his book and I was ready to be whatever help I could be. The first step was to meet the amazing woman who was instrumental in instilling the "attitude of gratitude" in Zane, his grandmother Carolyn. That meeting had an impact on my life that has changed so many aspects of how I live and reflect on each day. Carolyn and Zane buzzed with so much love, respect and spiritual energy that it was palpable in the air as we talked for hours. It was decided that I had both the heart and some skills that could be useful to Zane as he began the adventure of writing his book. For that, I am forever grateful.

It has been an honor to experience Zane's life "beneath the surface" of what the world has seen of him. His commitment to daily writing in his journal, morning and night, provides the fodder for incredible insights told in a rich style of story-telling. Hang on, it's quite a ride.

Shawneen Schweitzer: I have learned to never doubt my son when he says he wants to do something because I have learned that Zane really does "Believe and Create." I used to tell him often, "You have too much on your plate. Slow down, you're trying to do too many things. You can't do them all and do them all well."

Well, time and again he has proven me wrong. For example, when he got invited to the Ultimate Waterman, I thought, "How can you be good at all those sports? You have to focus on one. You're a champion in standup paddling." But, then he came home the victor in both 2016 and 2017.

I may have self-doubt that transfers to doubting what Zane can do, but he never doubts. He simply does what he's passionate about. The first time I really learned that was a time when Zane had just come home from a very long European trip. He would be home for just three days. This is typical of Zane. He had just been in Europe for many weeks and he was supposed to leave in 48 hours to go to Tahiti. To my surprise, that evening I heard a ding on my Facebook and saw a post that he had planned an InZane SUPer Grom Clinic down at Launiupoko in 24 hours. He wasn't even unpacked from his trip and he had made the post about the clinic. He had waited until the absolute last minute to make the post.

That was, at least, a sensible thing. We have learned that if we post about the SUPer Grom Clinics too early we will get 100 kids. His sweet spot is 25-30 kids. By posting it the night before, we get the perfect number of kids to make it safe and the best experience for all. When I saw the post on my phone I was really scared for him. What was he thinking? He is always traveling and never has any down-time for himself. The next day, Saturday, was his only free day at home before he had to catch a plane to Tahiti on Sunday. I was about to let him know what I thought but I realized it was the right thing to let him do what he wanted to with his short time home on Maui.

So, late Friday night, I was tired but I went to the market to get what was needed for the 30 goodie bags we always give the kids. We make posters for the kids. We put in granola bars and apples to keep the kids fueled in a healthy way. His sponsor Avasol gives us environmentally safe sun block and Honolua Surf Company gives us jerseys and reusable water bottles which the kids fill from a huge five-gallon jug we bring to the beach. Not using single-use plastic begins with showing them how easy a new habit can be built.

I woke up early that Saturday morning and Zane had already been down to the beach, had cordoned off the area and delivered 20 boards. Zane had brought 6 surfboards, 6 standup paddle boards, a couple of prone boards and two Starboard Starships. He had gotten all the paddles down there and had set up the tents. The clinic is usually 9:00 to 1:00 so we got down to the beach about 8:00. There were already close to a dozen kids there. The moment the kids noticed Zane had arrived they all began running toward him. They LOVE Zane. Suddenly all of my concerns about this being too much for Zane evaporated. I had an overwhelming sense of pride. I realized that I had to stop underestimating Zane's ability.

But that was just the beginning. As the day went on, more and more things kept happening. Each clinic includes a beach clean-up, a talk about the environment and the habit of using less plastic and recycling. The kids stretch and learn the various relays and events that will take place through the day.

While the kids were all down there participating in the activities, I noticed one child that comes to every event. She's Ava Heller, about 13 years old, with spina bifida. She cannot walk at all so she crawls or is wheelchair-bound. She comes every time and she trusts Zane. This event was about the fifth she had come too so she was getting more and more confident.

Zane went over to her and asked if she wanted to go on the board with him, and of course she did. He told her, "Today is the day we are going to surf standing up!"

She looked at him in disbelief, but from the look in her eye it was obvious she wanted to try. She said, "Okay."

All the parents were watching as they went out into the water. She was on the board, on a wave and Zane was holding her up. She was screaming with glee and we could all hear her from the shore. She looked like the girl from *Titanic* standing there.

When the wave died off Zane gently laid her down on the board, but you could see her pointing. She wanted to go again. She caught five or six waves with Zane. With each one we could see she was more excited and more confident.

Her father was on the beach with me and many of the other parents. I thought I was the only one crying at how wonderful this experience was, but I looked around and saw all the parents were in tears. Her dad ran up to Zane as he came in, ready to help Ava into her wheelchair. In typical teen fashion she cried, "No, Dad. Let Zane do it."

Zane carried her up to her wheelchair and told her that he was going to go surf with some other kids now. She grinned ear to ear, saying okay. The minute Zane walked away she looked at her father grabbing his face with both hands, pulling him toward her while exclaiming, "I was standing up, I was standing! I was really standing on the board!"

Well, that put us all in tears again. It was one of those experiences that I will always remember. My son made such a difference in this young girl's life, from her initial fear of even being on the board to being confident enough to let Zane lift her to a stand. She's gone on to represent Hawai'i in Special Olympics in swimming and inter-island surf competitions for Access Surf Hawai'i where she has to paddle lay down on the board and paddle her own prone surf board.

By 4:00, we were loading up everything after the event. We were the last people on the beach and I was exhausted. I looked over at Zane and he was just so happy. With tears in my eyes I told him, "I will never doubt you again. You just amaze me."

He was up until 3 am packing for his trip and we got him to the airport early. He told us not to worry, saying, "I can sleep on the plane. When I'm home I want to make the most of every minute."

I think that self-doubt or fear may be the reason that people don't do more. That was the way I was thinking, but Zane doesn't think that way. The impact of his can-do attitude is more powerful than a ripple. Some of the kids who have been coming to his clinics for years are beginning to do things for Maui Ola Foundation, sharing their talent and energy. One great example is Ty Simpson-Kane. He's become a great surfer winning many events. More importantly, like Zane always did as a kid, he has won the HSA "Aloha" award and volunteers at other events for less fortunate kids. (more on this topic in Chapter 7)

Matty Schweitzer, brother: From the day that my brother entered this world, it was pure, organic chaos in the best and most entertaining way possible. He has the energy, excitement and motivation of multiple pre-teens jacked up on caffeine, yet at such a young age he has the experience and wisdom of a 75-year-old lifelong world traveler. He is stubborn, hard headed and has his goals set for personal success. Yet he has the heart of a lion and will never make an excuse as to why he cannot lend a helping hand or change someone's life for the better. Zane truly wants to make this world a better place. Whether it's stoking out some kids on the beach or starting a non-profit organization to help take care of our Oceans, Zane is always doing everything he can for his community, family and the environment.

Very rarely do you meet someone who can talk the talk and walk the walk the way Zane does. From the crazy little kid with stitches all over his face and dozens of broken bones, Zane has continued his journey of self-improvement, success, inspiration and a true philanthropic lifestyle.

Do everything you can for your community and the people around you, don't make excuses and never limit your own expectations. That's what I get from Zane every day.

Connor Baxter, Multi World Champion Waterman, Fastest Paddler on Earth: How do I even begin to describe someone who has been not only a best friend to me but my closest thing to a brother. Zane Kekoa Schweitzer has the biggest heart of anyone I know and can make anyone feel the "aloha spirit" of Hawai'i no matter where in the world he goes. He is also one of the most talented watermen I have ever known. I look up to him in so many ways, both on and off the water. He has consistently pushed me and challenged me. That has helped make me into the athlete and person I am today.

Traveling around the world with Zane has never been boring. Zane knows how to make any situation instantly more exciting and his stoke never seems to run out. That's what I love most about him. He emits happiness everywhere he goes and always knows how to make even the worst situations better.

Perhaps our bond began because we share the same birthday. Or, maybe it was the blood bond we made after our first big fight. But since diapers, we have been together through it all. I am so lucky I get to call Zane my best friend and that each chapter of our lives has only deepened that friendship.

Svein Rasmussen, Founder and Chief of Starboard: Zane Kekoa Schweitzer lives an absolutely inspiring life story. That story is just starting to unravel through this book, which is sort of the first chapter. He can help create a better world through his curiosity, willingness to learn and ability to energetically share very important lessons. Zane is taking the lead in so many aspects and to work with him on anything is a lot of fun.

When stars align, special moments appear and guide one for life. Back in 1976, my father presented me a *National Geographic - Kids Edition* featuring a special story about a new sport called windsurfing. The story included an unforgettable photo of Zane's father, Matt Schweitzer, windsurfing into the sunset. My fate was sealed with that one shot. Yes, we are all one family across generations.

Judie Vivian, family friend and co-founder - Standup for the Cure: I have been a family friend of the Schweitzers for many years, and it has been a pleasure to watch Zane grow into the incredible young man he is today.

When we started Standup for the Cure early in 2011, Zane, who was only 17 years old at the time, eagerly committed to being its Global Ambassador and to heading up the "Zane Schweitzer Clinics." These clinics consisted of a team of Pro Athletes at each event with the role of introducing families to the growing sport of Standup Paddling.

The first Standup for the Cure (SFTC) event was held in Newport Beach, CA in May 5, 2012 where we expected 300 registrants and hoped to raise $30,000 for Susan G Komen to help uninsured local women get the breast health care and awareness they desperately needed.

Zane flew in with his family and stayed at our house in Seal Beach. Together, we watched as the numbers of registrants and sponsors grow exponentially. By May 4th, we had over 700 participants! Zane wanted to set a Guinness World Record for the largest SUP lesson ever and so we recruited the army reservists to come in full uniform to "police" the crowd and ensure a fair accounting of the activity per the Guinness guidelines.

He rallied his peers to serve as instructors and his brother, Matty, to film it all. Matty created a great documentary that told the story. The group included World Class Pro SUP athletes Brennan Rose, Matt Becker and Zane's sister Shelby. Together they followed his plan for this enormous lesson which was comprised of ten minutes of dry land instruction followed by twenty minutes of paddling on the water.

The evening before, Zane and his father Matt helped my husband Rob and our local volunteers set up ten corrals along the water's edge. This would enable the army reservists track the numbers of participants more easily. Zane then allocated one of his instructors to each corral.

The day of the event we all rose at 5:00am and set off to the event site to complete the set -up, Zane leading the charge with huge enthusiasm. As we drove down the coast toward Newport Beach, a huge cheer erupted in the van as the web site showed the donated funds raised were already tipping over the $30,000 mark.

As people funneled in through the registration area, Zane was like the Pied Piper magically attracting everyone to watch and follow his every move. Giving instruction and encouragement through a bullhorn, Zane orchestrated his Pro Instructors and, in turn, the class of over 500 standup paddlers. What a sight to see. They were all participating in the on-land instructions wearing matching SFTC pink shirts. Then en masse they launched onto the water. The incredible "Sea of Pink" was created as 500 pink-shirted paddlers launched in unison. That emotional moment brought tears to our eyes and goose bumps to our skin. A huge gasp erupted from the folk on the shore as such a sight had never been seen before. Cheers erupted all around with families hugging one another in amazement. The "Sea of Pink" led by Zane then paddled in a circular route around the bay to commemorate those who have lost their battle with breast cancer or melanoma.

Since setting the Guinness World Record for the largest SUP lesson, Zane has spoken about Standup for the Cure (SFTC) and the importance of early detection for both breast cancer and melanoma at competitions and in all of his interviews worldwide. His openness is breaking down the barriers for his peers in to talk about these diseases. He has donated his time and paid his own way to fly to almost every Standup for the Cure event since that inaugural event. As an example of his unending loyalty, he has had to make some serious detours from his nonstop global competition schedule. A few years back he was competing on the Standup World Tour (SUWT) pro circuit, and was confirmed to compete in France and then host his clinic a few days later at the Standup for the Cure event in Miami, Florida. But the SUWT had a last-minute competition addition to the tour that was to take place in Morocco.

Since Zane was in contention for the World Champion title he had to be at both events. All the athletes had just three days to get from France to Morocco to compete at the next big wave event. Since Zane had already committed to host the Zane Schweitzer Clinic in Miami he had to spend a good deal of money for the additional flight, log over 15,000 in airlines miles and spend way too many hours on the plane in order to make all three events. But he did it, that's Zane.

After successfully competing in the Standup World Tour event in France with an impressive 3rd place finish at the Standup World Tour, Zane raced from the award ceremony directly to the airport to hop on a plane and arrive in Miami the same morning as the SFTC event. After enthusiastically completing his popular clinic and participating in the event, he then raced back to airport just in time to board his flight to Morocco. He arrived in Morocco the same morning that the competition began. Zane traveled for more than 36 hours to spend 5 hours in Miami to honor the commitment he had to SFTC. This demonstrates the incredible personal sacrifice he is prepared to make for causes he believes in, and he does it all with a big smile on his face.

In 2017, SFTC reached $1 million raised to help 8,000 uninsured women get the breast health care they desperately need. The numbers tell the story. Since 1 in 8 women are diagnosed with breast cancer during their lifetime, he has been instrumental, with the SFTC team, in saving 1,000 lives.

Zane Kekoa Schweitzer spreads "Aloha" across the globe. He's truly inspiring to all of us.

My uncle Erik Aeder captured this moment – A wave ride at 3 years old at Launiupoko on Maui during the "Ole's Longboard Classic", where I had my first surf contest win!
Photo Credit: Erik Aeder

CHAPTER ONE

Beneath the Surface

My life has been a journey on and off the water. To most of you I am known as a waterman, a windsurfer, a surfer, a paddler. Just as underwater caverns, reefs and extreme rock formations hidden from our sight create the waves and the ocean's personality, there are hidden motivations, dreams, goals, choices and influences in my life that lie beneath the surface. In this book, through a collection of stories, people, events and life-practices, my hope is that you will discover what lies beneath the surface of Zane Kekoa Schweitzer, Ocean Enthusiast and Waterman. I hope this conversation will inspire you and shine a light on your unique story and path.

Throughout this book, the people in my family, in my community, among the teammates and competitors with whom I spend so much of my life, will be mentioned more than once. For now, here's just a short introduction to attitudes and philosophies that my 'ohana has instilled in me since I was very young. Those attitudes are like a deep ocean current, running powerful and constant through me.

Let's start at the beginning. I am 24 years old and proudly Hawaiian-born. I come from a long line of watermen and waterwomen. My grandfather Hoyle Schweitzer was an avid Malibu surfer in the 50's and met my grandmother Diane through bodysurfing. They eventually turned their passion into success when he invented the sport of windsurfing and drove its growth through all the ups and downs.

My father is a five-time World Champion and holds 18 world titles in windsurfing so you can only imagine the "catch up" I have had to do to be sitting at age 24 with 15 world titles. I still have to collect a few more to catch him. My mother was a nationally ranked women's windsurfing champion. They met while competing and traveled the world together for the sport they loved. Throughout their lives they have connected me and my siblings to both the ocean and to my roots.

My parents noticed early on that I had the passion to be one of the best watermen in the world. They had the confidence in me to believe that I could take a path similar to theirs if I applied everything toward that goal. Following in my parents' footsteps, I knew that if I trained hard and made the correct choices I could pursue my dreams as a professional waterman. I could travel the world just as my grandfather and father had done before me. I am so fortunate to be surrounded by love, support and an environment where reaching high and making a difference for others is nurtured.

I was given the gift of mindful reflection and "an attitude of gratitude" when my maternal grandmother Carolyn Jackson shared her practice of being actively grateful and present while encouraging my natural enthusiasm. The gift of being relentless with my dreams came from my grandpa Hoyle and grandmother Diane. They also instilled in me the importance and rewards of keeping a journal, riding the wave of opportunity and capturing the moment.

Three very different siblings make up our family. There's me, my older brother Matty and my younger sister Shelby. From Matty I learned to fight hard to be able to reach my goals. My brother is our protector. He cleared the path for us in Hawai'i. I consider myself the "Aloha," infectious vibration, and my sweet sister Shelby is pure inspiration. Shelby, who is two years younger than I am, taught me to enjoy the quiet moments and the importance of being confidently true to yourself.

Svein Rassmussen, founder and chief of Starboard, has been such an amazing influence on my life and the original "Dream Team" that consisted of Connor Baxter and myself. Svein started windsurfing in 1978 and won the Mistral Worlds in 1983. He was a gold medalist candidate for the 1984 Olympics and spent 10 years on the Professional Windsurfers Association (PWA) circuit. In 1991, he became the first sailor to win all disciplines in the IFCA production-board class Worlds. He believed in two eleven-year-old kids and ever since that time Connor and I have been traveling the world together. We started our career on the Junior World Tour for windsurfing.

Connor's parents, Karen and Keith Baxter, had been working with Starboard at that time. They are also both champion athletes. Karen was a world champion windsurfer and Keith was a champion Hobie Cat racer. As long as I can remember, Connor and I were windsurfing every chance we had and we were always connected to Starboard. Even so, for Svein who was running the largest water sport company out there to say, "Yeah, let's let these two Maui kids roam all around the world and represent my company and in return I am going to help support their dream. I am going to help them reach their potential," was amazing.

Who knew what vision, what belief in two stoked kids would bring. But knowing Svein "beneath the surface," as I do, it's that bold vision and risk-taking that has created the Starboard brand as the leader and the company taking eco-innovation to new levels. I have so much respect and loyalty for Svein. (More about this in Chapter 8)

I remember getting my first windsurf board, under the Christmas tree, signed, "From Svein." I knew that from that moment on I would be "Living the Tiki Life." Then along came the first standup paddleboards and I was among the first to get one from Starboard and try it out. From that early start, Connor and I just naturally started to excel in the standup paddling events. Slowly, more and more standup paddle events began to show up on the schedule around the world. I'm not one to pass up on an opportunity or the chance to follow an awesome lifestyle. Great things kept coming our way and all of a sudden, within a flash, Connor and I were traveling more for standup paddling than windsurfing.

It's crazy how these waves of opportunity come and go. It's probably happened to you. There are those times when you can "catch the glide" of something early and it makes all the difference. Connor and I made decisions at age ten or eleven and through our early teens that changed our lives forever. But we didn't do it alone.

Other gifts have come in unexpected places. For instance, a fellow Starboard "Dream Team" athlete, Sean Poynter, shared a book, *The Alchemist*, with me. Maybe you think of surfers and standup paddlers as always traveling, training and competing, which we do. But Sean, like me, is a pretty voracious learner. We have a deep drive to explore beneath the surface of powerful ideas and writings of great thinkers. There are hundreds of lessons and examples in the story created by Paulo Coelho. These two quotes inspire me and align with some of my core beliefs, "And, when you want something, all the universe conspires in helping you to achieve it," and "People are capable, at any time in their lives, of doing what they dream of."

Coelho also wrote, "Tolerance and compassion are qualities of fearless people." The gift and lesson of compassion and humility came from a trip to Peru, in a very poverty-stricken city. It was the same trip in which I won the Expression Session Junior World Title in Windsurfing in 2011. The real "win" went far beyond where I placed on the podium. I was in a community called Lobitos and it was a very poverty-stricken area with desert on one side of the town and a big beach with the beautiful ocean on the other side.

I remember walking through the town and seeing kids in the street playing soccer with trash. And one of the kids was just sitting on the ground in the dirt with no clothes on his back. He had no light in his eyes, no glow. He was just watching his friends play. For whatever the reason, he was watching without any interest.

I remember looking at him and just thinking, "Why? Why do I deserve to be here living like a rock star?" This kid was about my same age. Here I was following my dreams and yet there was this kid who didn't look like he had a fire in his heart for anything. I remember being really struck at that moment, on that trip, thinking, "I have to be able to not take what I am doing for granted. I have to be able to make the most out of my experiences and my opportunities."

During that trip, I began to realize that I wanted to share. The reason I had the opportunities that I did was because all my life I have been surrounded by a great learning environment; in Maui and with nature, with my parents, my brother's friends and the many people coming in and out of my house. There were so many I could look up to. I had the opportunity to learn from and be inspired by so many people.

We were already providing free surf lessons at events but I think that trip was special because I really saw why it was important to connect with the local community and give back. One way I could give back was to give clinics. That trip made me realize that what I am doing is for a much greater reason than just achieving results. I realized that I am at these events for a reason and I wanted to be able to use that platform for a greater good.

That trip my mom and I had packed a lot of coloring books, pencils and crayons from Maui to give to the kids when we visited a school. Then we participated in the event, the contest. After the contest, I donated a board and all the clothes I brought to the village kids. I left almost everything I had brought with me. After that we gave a free clinic. The most amazing thing was that most of the kids didn't know how to swim, even with the ocean right there beside their town. We had to teach them to swim before we could teach them surfing, or paddling, or windsurfing. Most of them didn't really get to surf or windsurf, but they were having fun in the water for the first time.

The best and most amazing thing that happened was that after this clinic there were actually kids playing at the beach. Before the clinic I didn't see even one kid on the beach. They were playing in the dirty streets. Yet, they had always had the ocean as a playground, open 24 hours a day, seven days a week right there next to them. They hadn't known or experienced it. But every day after the clinic for as long as I was there, we saw kids playing on the beach. They might have still been playing with trash or playing soccer with a can, but they were doing it on the beach. They were splashing and jumping in the ocean just having fun in the shore break. They had the board I donated and they were playing around with it. It was really rewarding for me. It was like I had given them keys to a playground they never even knew existed.

During that trip, I actually won the event. I remember we were celebrating afterward, having fun and a crazy time together. Ironically, one of the prizes I got for the win was a bottle of Pico Sour. It's an alcoholic drink that is pretty delicious, but we were just teenagers.

Of course, we thought it was time to celebrate. We were in a little town in the middle of nowhere, so we went to the beach where we built a huge bonfire. We got bored with that and took a ride in a truck. The game we played was crazy and dangerous. We were taking turns "surfing the roof." The driver would slam on the brakes and we'd go flying off the roof, just rolling into the sand yelling, "Let's do it again."

The next adventure we did that night was to take a hike up a hillside to a sea cliff to watch the stars and the moon. We were scrambling up toward the cliff and after that point I don't remember much of the night. That was because shortly after we got to the top of the cliff I slipped and fell. I fell about 30 feet to a small patch of sand barely as big as my body. All around me were jagged rocks. If I would have landed even a foot to either side the outcome would have been much worse. Luckily, my brother Matty, the team and two of the lifeguards from the beach were there. It took them a few minutes to get down to where I was, lying completely still, unconscious, with no breath and no pulse.

Here's how my brother Matty remembers that event, "Peru was a life changing trip for Zane and me. Zane was under age so he needed a chaperone. I was going to school in Australia and the event was during the beginning of my summer break. My mom wanted me to get the chance to travel more, so she asked me to go instead of my dad. In addition, she hoped that we would bond more by traveling the world together. When Zane was in Tahiti in 2011 I had been so bummed that I couldn't be there, instead I had been watching from my college dorm in Australia.

Another amazing aspect of the trip was that it was the first time I really took photos and videos. I had always messed around, but Zane had taken my Dad's really good camera with him. Since I had great equipment I started filming Zane that whole trip. It was the first time I was using a tripod rather than a hand-held. It was the first trip that we had done together without our parents and I really felt like Zane was almost an adult.

There were the most epic waves, windsurfing and kitesurfing, but the town was in the middle of nowhere. The arid environment of the area made Mexico look wet. There was not even a tree as we drove the three hours from the airport. We saw women walking for miles and miles with these huge jugs on their head coming from collecting water. Next came the sand dunes for miles and miles. Then, all of a sudden, we saw oil pipelines and pumps pumping. When we finally came over the last hill and we saw water – the coastline. But it was the first time I saw a coastline with no trees in any direction. It was so weird.

The competition was sponsored by Jeep so we had a Jeep to drive. The night after the competition we were driving around in the Jeep. There were no rules for under aged kids there, so the kids were taking turns driving. After a while we stopped in an open area that rose up a gently sloping hill. We decided to make a bonfire and hang out.

Behind us, near the bonfire, was this big hill. We really hadn't paid too much attention to it until Zane ran up to the top. He turned to call to us, took a step or two back, and we saw him go headfirst off the hill and out of our view. We imagined the hill on the other side was the same as this side and we would find him just rolling down a gentle slope.

We ran to the top of the hill and there was just a straight, sheer drop that was easily 20-30 feet down. Zane was completely lifeless, lying at the bottom. We couldn't even climb down to him. It was too steep. We had to go down the hill the way we came up and run around the base of the cliff to where Zane was lying. There were rocks all around him. Everyone's instant reaction when we saw him was that there was no way anyone could have survived that fall. We were sure he was gone. We got to him and he wasn't breathing and there was no pulse. I started doing CPR on him but they pulled me off. They made me stop. I was screaming, 'Wake up, wake up.'

The two older guys who were lifeguards continued doing CPR on Zane for a minute or two, then they stopped. They all gave up. He was dead. Everyone believed he was gone

I was lying on the ground with my head on his chest, and I was pray-ing to God, 'Just please God do something, I will change anything.' Then suddenly, it was the most amazing thing. Zane took this big deep breath, like a gasp, almost hyperventilating. It was like a jolt of life shot through him. It took about two or three minutes until he completely woke up. I was so emotional, shocked and relieved. I just wanted to hug him and tell him I love him but instead, the first thing I did was slap him. I was just so scared thinking we'd lost him. He kept trying to get up, to stand up, and he kept saying, 'I'm fine, don't worry.'"

Hearing Matty's perspective on what had happened to me that night still feels unbelievable. I don't remember anything about it. My mem-ory of the fall begins when everyone was hovered all around me. I was loaded onto a surfboard and Matty and some others began the drive of three or more hours to the hospital. We were in the middle of nowhere driving on roads that were bumpy and rough. At one point, we had to cross a rocky dry creek bed but Matty kept me lying on the surfboard as still as possible.

We arrived at a small run-down town where the hospital was prac-tically an open-air building, but they did have an x-ray machine to check out my back. Lying on the x-ray table I felt terrible, so beat up and nauseous. I was trying to communicate in Spanish that I was go-ing to throw up, "Donde esta el basura, the trash? Necessito el bano." It was just terrible, I threw up all over the nurses and the x-ray table.

The doctors didn't speak English and they seemed to be almost freaking out. But once we got the x-rays I learned I had just gotten a small fracture in my back, nothing more. We drove the many hours back to our surf hotel on the beach and arrived about 4 am. We slept just a few hours because at 6:00 we had to get up. It was the last day of the competition.

There is one last piece to this story. The day after my fall was the last day of the windsurfing competition. It was the "Expression Session," which was my favorite. It's a category in which all of the competitors go out at the same time and we are all on the same clock. It's usually where the best tricks, the most crazy stuff, goes down. It was a wave riding and jumping event, I love that. So even after the fall the night before I wanted to go do it, of course. I got really lucky since I hadn't broken anything in spite of how serious the fall was. I just tightened my harness over my black and blue back and finished the contest. I was in pain but my drive to compete was even greater. And – I won that day!

I remember going back to the place where I had fallen. Looking around at the area, I felt that I had been incredibly lucky. I realized that it had been nothing shy of a miracle. I couldn't help but wonder again, "How can I be standing here?" This was the same trip where I had first thought, "Why do I deserve this wonderful life and opportunities?" So much had happened and here I was contemplating a big question again, actually contemplating life, just living – period.

Then my thoughts went to my twin brother, Dane. You see, I was once "one of two." My mom had a third trimester miscarriage of my fraternal twin brother. She had never told me, yet somehow even at a very young age, I knew. When I was just shy of three years old I woke up from an afternoon nap and told my mother that I had just had a dream about my "other brother."

She asked me what I meant, "Do you mean Matty?" She said I was very determined and told her quite clearly "NO. Not Matty! My 'other brother,' the one just like me."

My mom must have been really freaked out because she ran and got my father. I told him the same thing I had just told her. After some back and forth my parents decided to tell me, for the first time, that I had been a twin. In an explanation simple enough for a child to understand they explained that only one baby was able to survive and that one was me. My twin had not developed enough and he didn't have enough strength to live so he gave it all to me, then he had gone to heaven.

My mom was crying, and Matty was quiet because he remembered my mom's pain at the time. Of course, I didn't remember. Mom and Dad still share the story of how I (at only 3 years old) just looked at them and said confidently, "I know." Now maybe it's that twin connection you always hear about, but he comes to me often in strange ways. He's with me quite often when I am in a dangerous situation. But he is always with me. I am a twin. He gave his strength to me, he gave his life to save mine. But I have often thought, "Why Me?"

I thought, if God still wants me here on this earth there must be a greater reason why. This thought came on top of feeling what I did while watching the young boy who was without a spark or fire of life. I remember wondering why I had gotten this second chance. I must be here to accomplish more than just getting results and being a competitor.

That trip really opened my eyes to living life for more than just myself. My experience as a teen, when I was struck with a sense of connection to a boy about my age who had nothing, made a deep impression on me. He had no clothes, no food in the belly, no love. These are some moments that I have never forgotten, that have stuck with me and that I carry with me every day. That trip gave me a shift that has inspired me to have a more compassionate, connected sense of life. I began to really search for and explore how and why can I use the opportunities that I have, not just for myself but for the benefit of those I come in contact with.

The deep currents that drive me to these adventures and endeavors are created by enthusiasm, passion and a strong belief of what is possible. In every chapter in this book it will become clear that I have been given the gift of incredible collaborators and mentors. One thing that has motivated me to strive for excellence is the people with whom I surround myself. We are the average of the five people we spend the most time with. I have learned, often the hard way, that when making decisions and going about life there's one thing we can control and that's the choices we make. The people we choose as friends, the routines and habits we choose to take on, or the attitude with which we choose to approach the day make all the difference. With every action, there is a reaction (thanks, Dad) so slow down and make your choices wisely.

As you join me in the journey that is this book, I hope that the stories inspire strategies and motivation to keep *your* inner fire burning. Keep feeding that fire with passion, positive energy and what brings joy to your life. It's easy to look at a successful waterman (or lawyer, or parent, or entrepreneur) and say the success was because they were at the right place at the right time. I don't ever want to take for granted or overlook the amazing teachers, mentors, learning environment, community or family that has all added to my "mana o" and success. But this life was not given to me, I had to work my okole (butt) off for it. I had to make sacrifices and I had to be relentless in my dreams by continuing to believe and create. I have had to adapt and grow in my own way.

Like you, I have had many challenges and obstacles. That's a given when you pursue a goal or dream. How do we react to those speed bumps on the road to success? I will share some stories and I hope they will remind you of your own ability to have grit and keep on pushing forward. Oscar Wilde once said, "Experience is simply the name we give our mistakes."

So, now that you have had a peek "beneath the surface" of Zane Kekoa Schweitzer let's continue the conversation. Until we meet a nd can talk story in person be relentless in your dreams. Remember what my Uncle Ron Hebert told me, "Success is when preparation meets opportunity."

Taking flight surfing on the Great Lakes, Chicago. With the help of a hydrofoil, surfing.
Photo Credit: Mike Killion

CHAPTER TWO

Innovate
and Inspire

As long as I can remember, my life has been built of dreams, goals, passion and inspiration. The best way I can think of sharing my journey is through stories: stories about a great day out with friends, a challenging obstacle that tested my abilities or an incredible place I've visited. We might not have all the answers, but we all have stories. Stories are all around us.

Stories connect us, make us feel alive, and inspire us. When your stories and my stories are shared, they become a personal and emotional experience to be remembered. It's my hope that as you dive into this book you'll discover stories that resonate. For more than a decade I have been writing my stories in blogs, event re-caps, magazine articles and journals. My journals have been an incredible tool to allow my memories to stay fresh and alive. It's a way to always have the ability to "learn from your past, live in your present and manifest your future."

It's been my intention to share these stories with the people I care about. Writing this book gives family and friends the opportunity to share the adventure and experiences with me.

We all have something in common no matter our age, our culture, our goals or our life journey. When we share stories together we feel connected with the people that are most important and valued in our lives. After work, after school, after an amazing adventure or goal met, one of the best parts is coming together and "talking story." Stories allow us to learn from one another, to reflect on what matters most, what we are proud of and what allowed our passion and purpose to really catch fire.

In this book, I will share some of my most treasured and private stories. You'll connect with me through the written history of the past decade of my life. While I'll be revealing my story, what I want to share is a practice that will allow *you* to record and create *your* stories too. In the process, your goals, values and beliefs will emerge in ways that can enhance your life – and even change your future!

We'll be going on a journey of journaling, a practice that has shaped and improved my life. Hopefully, you'll be inspired to explore a way to create your future through stories too because this is something that connects us all.

Obviously, I didn't have a conventional childhood. Early on I was extremely fortunate to feel the passion and have the drive to reach for the goal of being a world-renowned waterman. I had to sacrifice a lot to reach that goal. At age 11, I chose my career over the regular life of an adolescent. I was in 6th grade then and enjoying my first year at Maui Preparatory Academy (MPA). I missed quite a bit of school while pursuing my set passion and carrying the torch from what my parents and grandparents were equally passionate about – the ocean. I had my heart and head set on what I wanted to do for life, even at that young age. I aspired to be a world champion athlete, as both my parents have been. I strived to be believers and creators like my grandparents.

While traveling and competing, I missed many things that most people consider to be normal rites of passage for teenagers. But I didn't strive for normalcy. I strived for more! The high school curriculum became more demanding and my travel and training schedule grew. It became obvious that I would have to switch to an online high school after 9th grade.

I am very grateful for my time at Maui Prep and I carry this pride throughout my endeavors. My favorite classes were "The World and Its People," Japanese and Spanish. It's ironic because by the time I left Maui Prep after ninth grade I had already created a profession out of something I was most passionate about. I had traveled to over fifteen countries, had two world titles and had co-founded Standup for the Cure with my mother, Shawneen, my Aunt Judie Vivian and Uncle Rob Vivian, and our event organizer, Dan Van Dyke. Standup for the Cure is one of my proudest accomplishments having raised, by 2017, over $1 million dollars for uninsured breast and melanoma cancer patients.

It's completely natural that my passion in life revolves around time in the ocean. In, on or under the water I am my best self. I am a surfer who plays in the ocean, which has provided me with an enviable career. But while I spend a lot of time honing my skills on the ocean, I am not just a surfer. I am an ocean enthusiast. It's true that my life has been molded by the sea, but even more it's been shaped by the support, wisdom, love and connection with my family, my ohana, and my community in Maui. I've been immersed in the Hawaiian culture and traditions since birth.

I have been surfing since I could walk, windsurfing since about nine years old, standup paddling since I was thirteen and surfing big waves at places like Jaws and Mavericks since I was fifteen. Anything ocean related is a passion of mine. If I'm not surfing or windsurfing, I might be fishing, diving, tow in surfing, hydrofoiling or riding dirt bikes with my Dad and my older brother, Matty.

In many ways, my life has mirrored my father's. He started his windsurfing career in his early teens. His parents traveled year-round with him as they introduced and demonstrated windsurfing to the world. My parents had the privilege of being pioneers in the sport of windsurfing. They helped to make it into the sport it is today. My dad was the innovator of freestyle and big wave surfing. He was the first person to ever complete an end-over-end front loop in competition and went on to win eighteen World Titles. He reaped all the benefits that came along with being a pioneer and professional in the sport along the way.

I have also had the great opportunity to be an innovator and pioneer as well. Early on doors opened for me to refine my windsurfing skills and to prove to the world that kids could be as proficient at windsurfing as adults. Along with watermen Kai Lenny, Connor Baxter, Bernd Roediger, Kalani Hunt, Jack Golm and Baker Grant, I pushed my limits. Together we pushed the boundaries of our sport and our equipment. As kids, the summers allowed us endless time to invent tricks, and figure out what changes could improve our equipment.

When standup first came along, my sponsor Starboard wanted Connor and me to start bringing our standup boards with us to windsurf events for times when the wind was too light. Very quickly we started having a blast with our standup boards in the waves. In no time, we were doing tricks no one had considered trying. I was a short boarder and a skateboarder. I started trying tricks on the standup that I had used for surfing. It was just as much fun, except the boards were too big and too heavy. Starboard listened and innovated. Soon they started making smaller boards that were more progressive and the sport absolutely took off. After just a short time I was competing more on standup that I was on windsurfing. Everyone wanted to be a part of the new sport.

I feel proud to have been a pioneer in the sport of SUP and I know Connor and Kai do too. We broke down barriers, won world championships and pushed the level of the sport beyond what anyone imagined it would become. We helped the sport and the equipment progress along with our own progression. We inspired people all over the world, invented tricks, produced many incredible films and photo stories, all to help the sport grow. From a very young age, I was passionate about sharing my joy for the sports that brought endless opportunities to my life. This led to the creation of my InZane SUPer Grom Clinics™. I've had a blast getting other kids on the water and teaching many people all over the world surfing, windsurfing and even swimming skills. We are all now doing the same thing with SUP and windsurf foiling as well.

Laird Hamilton. Brett Lickle and Dave Kalama are the original "Ultimate Watermen." They were constantly changing it up and trying new sports, or re-introducing old ones. They were surfing new areas, bigger waves and were always doing new things. Without a doubt, Dave and Laird are the "fathers of standup." Brett Lickle is the "mad man" to first put a foil from an "air chair" on a surfboard which led to hydrofoil surfing. They were all pioneers in tow-in big wave surfing. They were our role models. We watched what they did and how they trained, then we did the same. We learned what it was like to be Professional Watermen, Innovators and Inspirers from Dave, Laird and the strapped crew including: Brett Lickle, Rush Randle, Pete Cabrinha, Robby Naish, Mike Waltze, Buzzy Kerbox, Victor and Gerry Lopez and, of course, my father Matt.

When I got my first foil from Alex Aguera at Go Foil, I instantly knew it would change my surfing forever. With the foil, I could surf the smallest wave for the longest amount of time. Foiling opened up a whole new playground and widespread surfing spots that no one without a foil could surf. This new sport allows for an escape from the hustle, bustle and ego of a lot of surfers and surf spots. Foiling gives the feeling of surfing while going for miles on the open ocean across a channel, riding swells that never break. It's an epic surf day every time. Imagine the feeling a pelican or sea bird feels when they glide low to the water riding the apparent wind from the ocean swells. Foiling gives me the sensation of flying. It is so serene.

I remember Starboard asked me to do a hydrofoil exhibition at the Pacific Paddle Games in Dana Point in 2016. It is probably the largest SUP Race in the world. Everyone was there. I decided to go out with Ridge Lenny and hydrofoil surf. All of our peers were in the water watching us. I got wave after wave from the very outside all the way across the beach to the shoreline. My brother, Matty, filmed it and posted it on Instagram. Within 24 hours we had over a half a million views. Everyone was interested in another new sport we were pioneering.

This year I was proud to be the first person to hydrofoil in a contest from Maui to Molokai across one of the world's roughest channels, the Pailolo Channel. Kai Lenny, Connor Baxter and Finn and Jeffrey Spencer were the first to complete a Maliko downwinder on a SUP hydrofoil. So, here we are at the beginning of another exciting adventure.

Don't be afraid to try new things. Many times, the path to success will change and curve, but as long as you stay on the course that includes opportunities to innovate and inspire you will undoubtedly have an adventure of a lifetime. Follow your heart because each day offers another chance to "innovate and inspire." Be bold, your potential is there if you go for it.

My brother, Matty, has pushed me to reach my potential more than any other person in the world. He and many of his friends are the world's best surfers. I was surfing and hanging out with surfing super stars like Dusty Payne, Clay Marzo, Kevin Sullivan, Wesley and Granger Larsen, Johnny Pitzer, and of course Matty, every day.

The way I remember some of our adventures when I was probably too young to be chasing Matty and his friends around is very different from the way Matty remembers it.

Matty likes to give this story as an example of what a wild and crazy kid I was, "We used to be really into BMX riding when we were kids. Right behind our house we had a full-on motocross track. We had no excuse not to be athletic. No matter what the conditions were, we had a sport to play.

If the waves were flat we went skateboarding or bicycle riding. There were no standup boards back then. If it was raining, we would play in the mud, have mud fights. We would still be biking in the mud or surfing the mud with our boogie boards. Even though we had all the newest video games and consoles, we never stayed inside long enough to play them.

My most vivid childhood memories are when I was 8 to 13 years old with Zane, who was five years younger than all of us, hanging out and trying to keep up. My strongest memories of him as a kid were at age 7, I don't know why that particular age sticks with me. He'd see us heading out and he'd come over with his sunburned scrunchy little face, and ask 'Hey, where ya going? Can I come? Please.'

We'd say, 'No, Zane, it's gonna be too gnarly for you.' And he'd always say that he could do it. One particular day stands out on my mind. Our neighbors had made these huge jumps in their yard. They were head high to us, the 12-year-olds, so they had to be way bigger than Zane. Even at my age, I was scared to hit those jumps on the bike, and some of my friends were too. We would do it, wearing a helmet and really getting mentally ready. We'd be so nervous when it was our turn to go. But just when you put your foot on your pedal to go, Zane would just come flying past you at your shoulder.

He was so little on this big red Mongoose bike way too big for him, peddling as fast as he could. We would see this little kid on this huge bike completely in the air. We had no idea if he did it on purpose or not, but he had his body flying up off the bike in this huge 'Super-man' position. We all wished we could do that. But he didn't have the strength to bring himself back to the bike so his ride always ended in a crash. That was just Zane.

That's where his nicknames all came from. My friends would say he's a little maniac, and then it morphed into Zaniac the Maniac, or Za-niac for short. Then we started calling him Insane Zane and then just InZane. He still lives life like that everyday which is why the nicknames all stuck. He's fearless and believes that if he tries hard enough he can do anything. The only difference is that now we all believe he can do it too."

Matty and his friends kept me scrambling and reaching high my whole life. We figured we would keep sharing our passion for sport, especially surfing in competitions, for life. Our plans shifted somewhat after a motocross injury sidelined Matty for about a year. Fortunately, another passion emerged for us to share. Matty travels with me whenever he can as my coach and mentor, my big brother and best friend. Togeth-er, thanks to Matty's photography and video talent, we have been able to capture our adventures together by taking video and photos of our crazy life and sharing them with the world. We post them on YouTube and Vimeo. They are on my You Tube channel, InZane's World YouTube Channel (the link is youtube.com/ZaneSchweitzer/ and Matty's chan-nel on Vimeo, Mat5o Media channels (vimeo.com/mat5o).

My life of traveling around the globe to events and competitions has allowed me to meet amazing people and experience many cultures and traditions. From the age of 11 most of my travel was with my close friend, Connor Baxter. We grew up together, and with friends like Kai Lenny, my brother Matty and his friends like Dusty Payne and Clay Marzo, we have always pushed each other. Through the years I strove for many goals along the way. Some goals were met, some eluded me. But I have the gift of being able to look back on so many experiences with fresh eyes and perspective because I have kept my journal for more than a decade.

I've been keeping a journal ever since I first started following the world tour for windsurfing back in 2006. My grandparents, Hoyle and Diane Schweitzer, gave the journal to me. Grandma Diane told me to write in it to keep track of all the fun adventures, special interactions and experiences, "Because when you get to be Grandpa's age it's going to be harder to remember."

It's amazing and entertaining to be able to always go back to your journal and recall your entries and moments. I already am so thankful to have kept track of my adventures and trips because for the last 5 years I have traveled to 15-20 countries each year for events. There have been so many amazing people and so many shared experiences. I know I wouldn›t have been able to remember them all without my trusty journal entries. They act as time capsules. Any day I can open a random day in any of my journals and immediately be taken back to the moment I was writing. I connect again with the environment that was around me, my feelings and experiences with the people I came across. It transports me back to the delicious spicy smells and sights in Morocco, to the shark infested waters of Reunion Island, to the sweltering heat of the dense Brazilian jungle.

Writing in my journal is now a natural part of my day. In the beginning, it took some serious effort, especially when I was a teenager. The hardest part was sitting down and starting to write. Once I picked up my pencil and journal the rest came easy. Having my journals is not just about being able to recall my stories, but also to remember the hardship and gratitude I've experienced along the way.

My journal contains my history and a wealth of stories. I know that like special moments in life, stories are best shared with friends. So, through this book I will share my stories with you. My hope is that they will resonate with you whether you are young or old, a surfer or not.

There is a life purpose ready to be discovered whenever we use our gifts and talents to respond to something we believe in, something larger than our personal goals. My sense of purpose, passion and knowledge didn't come to me all at once. It came slowly over time. My mother instilled in me the philosophy of making every moment count and taking advantage of every opportunity that presents itself with positivity. I have always followed that advice. My Dad taught me to be active every day toward your goals. He taught me that with every action there is a reaction and, if every once in a while I need to remember to be humble, "Make sure that helmet fits."

Just like you, I have some unique gifts. As I documented my life story, strong threads and themes have carried throughout. Remembering and reflecting on these themes have helped me make better use of my gifts – and my time. This book is an invitation to you to join me on a journey toward mindful gratitude and creating days that are amazing. Along the way you will discover your purpose, gifts, passions and values that are right there for you.

"Innovate and Inspire" is my personal mantra. Through a collection of my stories you'll be right there with me through the years as I searched for and discovered innovation and inspiration every day. When you have a job like mine, people often think it's all fun and fame. It can be. But traveling constantly often brings overwhelming challenges, stress and interruption of routine. Training full time is demanding. Competition is stressful and the traveling required is exhausting. It takes a toll on your body. Journaling is a routine that keeps me focused and grounded no matter what travel, competitions or life sends my way.

My journals give me a checklist, actions and a way of thinking that keeps my eyes on the prize, my head in the game, and my heart in the right place.

My journals provide daily reminders to write down things for which I'm grateful, ways I will make my day amazing and ways I could have improved my day. Over time I am actually creating a life that is well-lived. Writing the innovation and inspiration I discover each day has made an impact on my decisions. In a way, I have been visualizing my goals and taking a step toward reaching those goals every day through my consistent practice of writing and reflecting.

The people, experiences and cultures we encounter create so many stories. I would have forgotten many of these if I hadn't written them down. Now I keep three journals. I have a *Five Minute Journal* from Intelligent Change that invites me to write short entries and focus on each day. The *Five Minute Journal* is well-designed by Intelligent Change co-founders Alex and UJ. They distilled UJ's 30-minute journaling practice into a simple, quick journal to help people become happier, have space for reflection and appreciate life more. Best of all, even the busiest person can build a habit of daily journaling with the prompts and guidance of the *Five Minute Journal*.

The second journal is my "devotion journal." In that one, I write longer observations and thoughts, often while I'm at an event or during my travel back home. I take time after trips and events to reflect and write in more detail. The stories that end up teaching me powerful lessons aren't always obvious while I am living them. I also keep a "Performance Journal." This journal is for my career as a waterman. It allows me to track my training, results, the equipment I use in different conditions and such.

Life can be chaotic. It doesn't matter whether we are chasing world titles, striving to change the world or just surviving through life day to day – we all need to overcome obstacles. Like me, you probably puzzle about why we are here and how we can discover the innovation and inspiration to live our best life. The stories we tell ourselves have a way of focusing our energy and inspiration. Re-reading my stories, I am amazed at what is revealed. So often I discover by re-reading a journal entry that victory in a competition hasn't resonated as strongly as the interpersonal connections that grew from the experience I had.

Over time I became inspired to find ways to connect with the people and cultures I was blessed to experience around the world. I always immerse myself in the people, culture, language and lifestyle when I travel and try to imagine and feel what it's like to be in the shoes of the locals. In turn, I have committed to keep my own culture alive in me and for generations that follow. Recently, I had a new goal. I knew "what" I wanted to do. I wanted to learn more of the Hawaiian language. I knew "how" to do that. But it wasn't until I had a really powerful reason "why" I would learn more of the Hawaiian language did I really gain the inspiration and focus.

Getting to the "why" makes all the difference. "Ke aloha nui iā ʻoukau pākahi a pau." This is one of my favorite Hawaiian quotes which I learned after committing to taking on a study of the Hawaiian language. Its meaning is, "So much love for each and every one of you." The spark, the "why do it" for that commitment, came with the birth of my beautiful niece, Sage. I sourced that phrase by asking a fluent Hawaiian-speaking friend for a translation of the words, "love for you all." I wanted to share that quote with my family and baby Sage at a family dinner "pule," or prayer.

Once inspiration is part of the process, other remarkable things begin to happen. That same phrase popped up in my journal when I was writing about the 2016 Ultimate Waterman competition and my life-changing experience of connecting with the Maori people, competitors of the Ultimate Waterman who turned into great friends and elders in New Zealand. I wrote those words in my journal, "Ke aloha nui iā ʻoukau pākahi a pau!" I wanted to share my heartfelt gratitude and love for the people and the wisdom they shared.

I wrote in my journal, "These are the moments that last. I am feeling so blessed and grateful for all the aloha and mana we have all shared and experienced here with each other. You all are inspirational and it's been an honor to learn from you all and share each other's manaʻo (knowledge and beliefs)!"

Discovering innovation and inspiration may not happen in a sudden "aha" moment. With the discovery of a great idea or success of a goal met, there is usually a long period of time between the first notion and the time of attaining it. Have you ever had a goal that seemed almost impossible? I've had so many goals that could've fit this description throughout my life, but I never looked at these goals as impossible. I've always aimed to shoot for the moon, since the worst that might happen is to fall amongst the stars. At the time of setting the goal I might not have been ready to discover the best path or solve the problems around meeting it, but I can bet you that I approached the goals I did accomplish with passion and inspiration from start to finish.

Here's an example of a huge goal I had and the surprising way doors opened to me when I least expected it. All my life I have worked towards becoming a true waterman. What better way to learn than to be part of The Ultimate Waterman Team. The Ultimate Waterman is an annual challenge of eight ocean sports presented to eight of the top watermen in the world. The sports include outrigger (OC-1), prone paddling, SUP surf, long and short board surfing, SUP racing, underwater strength-endurance challenge, and if the waves are big enough then they will have a big wave event as well. There could be few other places in the world with the coastline, countryside and diversity of environments as perfect for hosting this event as New Zealand. It is similar in many ways to Hawai'i but more cold, rugged and extreme.

I was a late invite for the 2016 event, receiving the invitation only two weeks or so before the event. At the last minute, my close friend and 7X World Champion Waterman, Kai Lenny, could not attend and I was the first alternate. This meant that I was more unprepared mentally than the others guys. I figured I had nothing to lose. I just needed to give it my all, have fun, feel the humility and learn in the areas I didn't have 100% confidence.

It helped a lot to be going to the event with Connor Baxter who's a Starboard teammate with me and like a brother. Connor and I have been best friends since before double digits. He's one of the most talented, humble and loyal people I know. We have been traveling the world together on the windsurf world tour since 2005. We both juggle preparing and training for multiple world tours. Our experience has brought us to so many amazing places and people, not to mention what we have already achieved together and independently in competition in the windsurf and SUP world. Connor is literally the fastest paddler in the world and eight-time Racing World Champion.

Connor was the first person I called when I heard I had been selected. He was stoked and gave me the low-down, lots of advice and helped me prepare and pack according to what everything was like the year before. We are the original Starboard "Dream Team" and it was epic to travel to the event and represent Hawai'i together.

We came to the event as individuals, competing for the honor of earning the title, Ultimate Waterman. From the very first day all eight of the competitors lived together, ate together, and slept in the same quarters. We were fully immersed in both competitive events and the culture of New Zealand. On the very first day of the Ultimate Waterman events, there happened to be a festival celebrating Polynesian cultures in Auckland very near to where I was. It was the Pasifika Festival. It was very important to me to be there to experience it. There was a team from Hawai'i sharing the Hawaiian culture and I was blessed to be able to speak at the festival. I had the opportunity to share stories about the Ultimate Waterman; who we are, what we do, and how we respect the skill set of each athlete.

As I stood there alone on the stage, one of the Maori leaders offered a blessing to me. She said, "I mua a e lei i ka lei o ka lanakila," which means "move forward and encircle yourself with the lei of victory." Then she repeated, "I mua Kekoa, i mua," and invited the entire crowd to repeat with her. "I mua Kekoa, i mua!" "I mua Kekoa, i mua!" The meaning of I mua is "move forward."

When the entire crowd chanted that blessing to me it was so strong, so chilling. Being connected to a community, to a culture so like my Hawaiian culture from home, I felt blessed and honored. It made me feel I was on the right path all the way in New Zealand. Not just the right path for me, but also for my community and for my family.

Let me ask you, "Have you had such a moment? Have you had a moment when what you have been working toward with all your heart and passion is acknowledged by a larger community that honors and respects your journey?"

It was like that for me at that moment in New Zealand. It was so powerful. The moment made me feel that what I had been working toward my entire life was right and true. My life, my lifestyle, consists of many steps in a long journey. Giving and getting support through connections, so many friends, family and mentors along the way, has motivated and inspired me through that journey. Just as I've had the privilege to learn from other watermen: from the Maori in New Zealand, from my community in Hawai'i, from my family, you have probably also had inspiration and support that brought you to a spiritual motivation. Hopefully as I share my story, it will remind you of your own strong and true connections in your life.

There are cultures, mentors and people with vast wisdom gained through experiences that we might never have connected to if we had not been open to it. Staying on the lookout for innovation and inspiration throughout your days, throughout your life, you will discover what you need. I encourage you to take the time to be mindful and to write down your experiences too. You will be constantly surprised at what you discover from what you choose to write.

The loftiest dreams and the biggest life goals are built from a foundation of choices. Everyday choices and your collection of everyday attitudes create a map of your journey and your progress toward your true passion and purpose. Here's an example. The night I made the choice to attend the Pasifika Festival I had invited all of the other athletes to go with me. They made the choice that was right for them after the first day of a tough competition, knowing there was even more coming up during the next eight days. They all passed on going to the Festival. But for me, there was an undeniable desire to go and to experience the people, the culture and the Festival. I followed my heart, and went without my teammates. As it turned out, I had one of the most powerful moments of my life. "I mua Kekoa, i mua!" I mua – there is such power in following your heart and intuition, in moving forward.

For many years, I have looked back and said, "This has been an incredible year." Over time I have really seen my training pay off. That is what every athlete works for. When I came away from the Ultimate Waterman competition as the champion, it was an incredible honor for myself, my family and my Hawaiian community. It's amazing to think that in 2010 I won the Stand Up World Tour at Sunset Beach, Hawai'i in the Junior Division. Two years later I won my first World Title on the Pro Tour at Honoli'i Bay on the Big Island and it has just kept going from there. Throughout this book I'll share plenty of exciting stories about events, training and travel. As you read, let your mind wander and remember the stories that have created *your* journey and created a pathway to *your* success.

It goes to show that if you love what you are doing, dream big, train hard and go for it, you can do anything. Whether you're in business, a student, or are striving for excellence in a sport, once you really get to know *why* you aspire for your goals, the journey becomes more incredible.

Innovation: Each of us has the ability to take risks, which is really what innovation is. The bigger the risk – the higher the reward. We have the capacity to discover new ideas and big goals wherever they emerge. But without impact, innovation is just an idea with promise. How can we inject more innovation into our lives? The process doesn't have to be life-altering. Over time, be open to seeing ways to break from previous practice. Give different elements, ideas or choices a try, use your imagination and listen to ideas that might differ from your own. Innovation will discover *you*. *Your* ability to "innovate and inspire" will emerge.

Talk about different elements and ideas making an impact, movies are an incredible way to combine images, action, music and innovative stories. I have been really fortunate that I was included in so many movies, like *The Progression Project, The Sup Movie, H2Mexico, Don't Crack Under Pressure II and III, Risky Business, That First Glide, StandUp Paddle Movie, The Starboard Movie,* and many more. My adventures have also been featured on many television shows including the Xterra Planet *Surf Adventures* television show, Xterra Sports Adventure

Series, CBS Sports Network's *The Ultimate Sup Showdown*, *The Backdoor Shootout / Pipeline*, *2016 Pacific Paddle Games* and Red Bull TV's 3-show series on The Ultimate Waterman 2016 and 2017.

My brother, Matty, (Mat5o Media) captures story in a visual way, through photography and video. Matty has been living, eating and breathing action sports since the day he was born. Like me, he surfed before he could walk, was dirt biking by the age 4 and was the first ever third generation windsurfer. Matty and I train and travel the world together. His video and photos inspire me. He's taught me to discover so much when we look over the images. Innovation isn't always about something new, but discovering it through new eyes or from a new perspective. So often when I write in my journal I have been influenced by Matty's ability to capture the unique essence of beauty in everything life has to offer. Matty has also been my coach, guiding me with video surveillance and training.

As you discover ways to include innovation and inspiration in your life I hope you can connect with people whose perspective is different from yours. See life through the eyes of others, hear their stories and allow yourself to grow.

How can you bring innovation to the world? For me that practice begins with remaining enthusiastic, authentic, improving and providing value every day. It's not the one big, dramatic event that drives innovation. In a way, by constantly seeking innovation we get regular nudges toward the growth and improvement that really matters.

Inspiration: Inspiration is the driving force fueling our dreams and goals. Inspiration lies everywhere. Sometimes we look so hard for inspiration that we just don't see it. My practice of writing at the beginning of the day sets me upon my day with an open, wide-eyed sort of energy and spirit. At the end of the day I reflect, guided by the prompts in my journal. Inspiration has often found me right there, reflecting on the day's path that I chose.

My family and I started Schweitzer Sports Foundation when I was 12 years old. We have always believed that you should give back to those less fortunate. As I have traveled the world I have met many kids in need. I have been able to donate my time, money, clothing, sporting equipment, books and toys to children in need. Giving back is rewarding. One of the most rewarding programs to donate time to is Duane DeSoto's Naka Kama Kai (Na Kama Kai) organization during APP World Tour stops with all the other pros, or when I organize free ocean safety, surfing, swim and SUP lessons for the kids wherever I travel. I have taught many children from all over the world, including Peru, Brazil, Mexico, Thailand, South Korea, Japan, Italy, Morocco, Dubai, Dominican Republic, France, and of course, right here in America. Many of my friends will join me in teaching the clinics. We all seem to have as much fun as the kids. I always try to donate some of my used equipment when I leave so that the kids can continue to experience the joy of the ocean.

My mother, Shawneen Schweitzer, co-founded Standup for the Cure with our family friends, Judie and Rob Vivian, myself and Dan Van Dyke. It began as a little idea discussed on the beach meant to honor Judie's fight with breast cancer and as a way to start a conversation with others. Judie Vivian is a force to be reckoned with. She truly lives life to the fullest, with passion and a relentless pursuit of excellence in everything she does. I have the honor of being the event's Global Ambassador. That experience has enriched my life in many ways.

At Standup for the Cure (SFTC) events I host free SUP clinics for breast cancer survivors and their families at an ever-growing number of cities. As of summer 2017 we have raised over $1,000,000 for breast cancer research and set the Guinness Book of World Records for the largest Stand Up Paddle lesson ever taught. While it's great knowing that every $125 raised will allow a person to receive a breast cancer screening and raise awareness, the most inspirational part is the people. Paddlers are often survivors out on a standup board for the first time. Teams and families paddle together to support someone fighting breast cancer or in memory of a loved one. The energy is electric with smiles and hugs everywhere. We create a community through a fun, easy to learn activity such as SUP. This allows the opportunity for comfort and confidence to share whatever it is we are going through with our loved ones.

Our SFTC Health Expo also offers free breast exams and skin exams to all participants. We have done over 1,000 exams and helped to detect breast cancer or melanoma in 21 people (as of early 2017). Our mission statement, "Have fun and save lives," is legit and extremely inspirational.

Being open to the magic of inspiration will make you stronger in all aspects of your life. You don't need to be anything but your true authentic self. Just trust your instincts. By being mindful, sort of having your eyes open for inspiration, you'll discover how often it's present. Why do you do what you do? Once you know "why," the what and how will be easy.

By writing down the presence of inspiration as it happens in a day, you are able to keep it for future use. How often you have listened to your heart as you reflect on the inspiration you've discovered? When you have recognized a particular moment or experience being filled with inspiration, believe it is the right thing for you, right now. Whenever you do things, or wherever you go, go with all your heart!

My grandparents have always taught me that "your life is a beautiful thing. Make the most of it by finding inspiration wherever you can." It amplifies your happiness and impacts how you engage with the world around you. Steve Jobs says it like this, "Have the courage to follow your heart and intuition. They somehow already know what you truly want to become." Bring your journal out at the end of the day and actually write down what made your day special. What could have made it more amazing? Specifically, what actions or changes could you have put into motion?

The most ordinary days sometimes deliver the best inspiration. I am always ready to hop out of bed for the early morning "dawn patrol" and from time to time my sister, Shelby, motivates me to go. Shelby and I are just over two years apart in age and we are very close. She is so much more than an athlete. She's an artist, a musician, a poet, an environmentalist, an animal lover and introspective in her ways. While she has been a Hawai'i State Champion and a US National Champion both in surfing and standup paddling, surfing is also her quiet place, her place of comfort. I love that she has opened my eyes to the value of the "quiet moments." I have a lot of energy and a different pace than Shelby has. Those differences balance perfectly when Shelby and I share our time together on the water. I have lots of stories with her but I am choosing to share two very simple entries from my journal that she instigated. Simple days, for sure, but ones I will always hold close to my heart. These were ordinary days that could have become a blur in my memory but stay fresh and fun because I wrote about them.

On January 12, 2016 I wrote, "Today I got one of the best barrels of my life on a longboard. Shelby has been wanting to surf Windmills more lately. It can be a very challenging surf break so, she asked me to go with her early this morning. We went on our own, leaving (our friend and filmmaker) Guy Mac, Matty and Matt Bromley (a big wave surfer from South Africa and the star of Guy Mac's movie, *Risky Business*) at home. We were on a fun dawn patrol together. Shelby caught a few fun waves and, most importantly, got comfortable in the lineup. I had a GoPro with me and I got a rad shot of local grom Eli Hanneman and Shelby on a great wave together.

We went home and ate lunch. Then we helped my Dad move a stove and refrigerator out of our Kahana house with Guy, Matt and Matty. After this we went to Choice Health Bar for acai bowls. Next, we went bottom fishing off the SUP boards. Guy caught a good-sized yellow spot papio and was super stoked. Later, about an hour after sunset, I hooked up a small uku too. That uku gave me a super fun fight."

Five Minute Journal entry January 12, 2016

1 / 12 / 16

Today I got one of the best barrels of my
life (on a long board)! Shelby has been interested
in surfing windmill lately & she asked me to go w/
her early this am. We went in our own
& left Guy, Matty & Matt and just went for a fun
dawn patrol together. Shelby caught a few and
most importantly got comfortable in the lineup.
I had a gopro w/me & got a rad shot of Eli kamman
& even one of shelby!

Went home, made lunch, helped dad moving
stove & fridge out of Kahana house w/ Guy,
Matt, & Matty. After this we had Choice Health
Bar Acai bowls then went bottom fishing off the
SUP boards! Guy caught a epic good sized
yellow spot papio & was super stoked. I was a little
jealous at 1st b/c it would have been my biggest papio
off SUPs yet! After 1 hour maybe still no
bites since then, do dark after sunset I hooke
a small VKV which was a super fun fight!

A regular day, right? But I'm so glad it wasn't forgotten. The other dawn patrol day I had with Shelby I also got to ride some big barrels. Maybe she is my lucky charm! The day was November 6, 2016 and in my *Five Minute Journal* I wrote that I was grateful for the clear beautiful stars I can see from my bed, for my sister motivating me to go on dawn patrol with her and for my brother waking up early to go with us. I anticipated what would make the day great and included, "getting barreled, seeing the boyz and friends in the water and organizing around the house."

Like I do each morning I wrote an affirmation. Today's was, "I am determined and inspired."

Five Minute Journal entry from 11/6/2016

Ahupua'a & Cultural Practices educational center

☼

DATE 11 / 6 / 2016

*Seek constant, critical feedback. If you don't know how
you're doing, you won't know what to improve.
Focus ruthlessly on where you need help.*

DANIEL PINK

I am grateful for...

1. For the clear beautiful stars I can watch from bed
2. My Sister motivating me to Dawn Patrol w/ her
3. My brother waking up early to join us.

What would make today great?

1. Getting barreled
2. Seeing the boyz & friends in the water
3. Organizing around house

Daily affirmations. I am...

I am determined & inspired...

Met w/ Torsten to introduce Hoku & collaborate together for my
vision of creating a educational center for comunity focussing on Hawaiian
values & practices...

3 Amazing things that happened today... help Hawaii &

1. Got the ball rolling for an amazing project that can its PPl big time
2. Learned a lot from Hoku on Hawaii language, history & legends.
3. Organized/got all my gear safe in my new container!!
4. Surfed Honolua & got to coach Shelby...Recived aloha & complimcnts
from Augie & uncle Roy!

How could I have made today even better?

By getting 100% packed so I wasnt rushing.

As I reflected while writing that night, the day had been great on so many levels. I got to surf Honolua with Shelby and coach her. I received aloha and compliments from Augie and Uncle Roy. I did organize, and packed my new container with all my surf gear in preparation for the 2016 ISA Worlds in Fiji. I learned a lot from my friend Hoku Haiku on the Hawaiian language, history and legends. That reflection aligned so well with many of my aspirations and goals around that time.

That same day I had a chance to introduce Torsten Durkan to Hoku Haiku. Torsten is another Maui friend of mine and he started a foundation to motivate pro athletes to "give back" through his non-profit, Surfers BeCause. I introduced Torsten to Hoku for a collaboration meeting on a project that is very important to us all. It involves education and a community center focusing on Hawaiian values and practices that could help the future generations of Hawaiians.

From that one day, I don't know what the future holds but the day was full of innovation and inspiration. It was truly an amazing day. Is "amazing" a word that you use to describe many of your days? It is a mindset that is closely connected to "Innovate and Inspire," to be inspired and inspire others. Imagine back over your day and find the amazing moments no matter how inconsequential or small they might have been in the scope of the BIG picture. They are each your treasures, your amazements and most valuable when you reflect on them and write them down.

There is a Hawaiian word I often bring to my mind, the word is manaʻo. The word reminds me of the importance of respect, mindfulness and the Hawaiian value of manaʻo. Manaʻo is not just knowledge, but it is also the acknowledgment and appreciation of the knowledge, mentoring or energy that has been shared. For example, when I learned a paddle stroke technique from legendary waterman Dave Kalama that influenced my paddling in training or competing, I acknowledged and respected where that manaʻo or lesson came from. I am grateful for what Dave has passed on to me. I am aware of what that manaʻo has brought to my life, whether it be with a result or added comfort on the water.

We have a tradition in our family that began when my mother thought it would be a good idea to take time in the evening to share with each other what the best part and the worst part of our day was. We talk about how we might have changed something. We still do this when we are together at our family dinner table. Those are just a couple of examples of so much mana'o I have received from so many people throughout my life. Their innovations and inspiration fuel my desire to keep that energy flowing.

You might think to yourself that there isn't necessarily any connection between the things you write while reflecting on your day and the day's eventual outcome. What could come from listing what would make a day great? How could that impact the actual outcome of the day? It happens! A pattern will emerge over time in the list of items you write in the evening that actually *were* amazing aspects of your day. It's all part of building an openness to opportunity, inspiration and developing our mindfulness so we create our best life experience.

Before closing your journal at the end of the day, look back on all those hours and think about what you might have done to make the day even better. Look at your shortcomings, mistakes, attitudes and actions square in the eye. Without blame or self-degradation, simply state how you might have made your day better. Your openness to examining a day in this way is a great treasure for learning and can bring you optimistic hope for days in your future. You will also find that it discourages procrastination as well. Since you are writing it down you are giving it importance.

Rather than shoving thoughts away without examination or awareness, we create a collection of days wide open to discovering and sharing innovation and inspiration. An investment of a relatively small amount of time at the beginning of the day and powerful reflection at the end of the day makes all the difference.

Be prepared for what's ahead of you and act in your present.
I'm enjoying being home to surf my favorite wave at Punalau.
Photo Credit: Dooma Photos

CHAPTER THREE

Every Step Matters

Where do you hope your journey in life will lead you? Whether your "steps" are across the miles, toward a goal, a relationship or beyond a challenge – each one matters. Lao Tzu's wisdom is often quoted, "The journey of a thousand miles begins with one step." As true as that is, it can also be said that the first step is the hardest to make. Sometimes you need to just go and not linger on the thoughts that are holding you back.

Our journey made of millions of steps and thousands of life-miles is rarely a straight line in the direction we hope for. Just like all the corrections a waterman makes following the wind and currents during a paddle crossing through the Ka'iwi channel or the fluid moves and corrections made while surfing the face of a wave, what's important is to constantly be in the moment and adapt. On the path that we choose to follow in life, we often come across obstacles. Each obstacle and how we choose to get past it makes us stronger. Each step on our life journey will lead us across challenging valleys and up some hills that seem pretty daunting. "Be Relentless" with your dreams.

A philosophy that I keep in mind during the ups and downs is summed up as, "Every Step Matters." It is the mission statement from Cobian Footwear. I am proud to live by this mission statement and to be a global ambassador for Cobian. I am honored to also represent companies with similar missions that align with my beliefs. I love Cobian because they value community influencers and giving back to the community as much as they value our athletic achievements.

What does "every step matters" mean? For me, each day starts with a plan of attack. Each action I take towards that plan is like a step.

Every day I make so many choices and through them the days unfold. Throughout the day, steps can be made toward my plan. These steps are either created through innovation and inspiration, or lead away from my plan through distraction. My choices made each day bring me closer to a goal – or not. Reflecting on my day allows me to really think about the steps I chose and to be grateful for the opportunity to learn, grow and create the life journey that's best for me. I've read before that if you're not growing, you're dying. I'd prefer to continue growing. Through the choices and steps made daily we can grow closer and closer to our desired outcomes.

That statement is so important, so let's hear it again, "Reflecting on my day allows me to really think about the steps I chose. Looking back over the day helps me to be grateful for the opportunity to learn, grow and create the life journey that's best for me."

The day's choices and actions are steps that matter, but reflecting on the day and living in an "attitude of gratitude" are also steps that matter as much. At the end of the day when I write in my journal I get a second chance with how I think about the steps and choices that made the day. No one is perfect, but with this practice we can learn to become aware of our mistakes and embrace the lesson of being humbled by targeting our flaws or mistakes. Each day offers the chance to avoid the same or similar mistakes in the future.

Gratitude journaling is a starting point. Just like practicing awareness of confidence and purpose is powerful, so is acknowledging gratitude. Every time you write in your journal you give yourself an opportunity to go back and reflect on what happened. You get a chance to see things from a different perspective. This habit becomes a step toward discovery – and the potential for a story you'll treasure over the years. Every Step Matters!

Thought power is the key to creating your reality. Everything you perceive in the physical world has its origin in the invisible, inner world of your thoughts and beliefs. What we think and what we think about, we become. One habit that can help any of us become the master of our destiny is being keenly aware of our strongest and habitual thoughts. By doing so, you will be able to attract into your life your most true intentions.

The following words of Siddhartha Gautama Buddha perfectly capture the essence of thought power, "All that we are is the result of what we have thought. The mind is everything. What we think we become."

I do believe that what we invest our thoughts on and our energy toward manifests our reality. My life has been filled with many blessings and experiences. I know these blessings and opportunities will continue coming to me and my loved ones. I am inspired and "manaiakalani" (drawn toward) ho'oponopono. What is ho'oponopono?

Ho'oponopono is an ancient Hawaiian method of reducing stress and problem solving through a form of affirmation and forgiveness. The word ho'oponopono means to make things right. It's a Hawaiian practice based on manifestation. The way I understand it is that everything you come across has energy that can either come along with you or be cleaned away. Like a computer, if there is information overload the system will run slow. The job you're doing will be delayed because of everything else working in the background. Everything that happens to you comes from what you focus on in your mind. If you don't clean the thoughts or energy, even if they are subconscious, they will take away from your direct conscious thought process. To ho'oponopono is more than just making something right, in a way it is almost like clearing your slate and learning how to feel a fresh start with a clear mind.

I am deeply passionate about Hawaiian traditions and the practice of manifestation. The form of the practice I use is a system I am learning from the book taught by Dr. Ihaleakala Hew Len. I am not an expert in the practice so I practice to the best of my abilities right now. I was inspired to practice this more by a friend, Ni'iloa Kamehameha shortly after taking on the stress and emotions of losing my beautiful cousin, Justine Clawson, after she was tragically murdered at just 23 years of age. We were so close and I loved her very much. The loss our family suffered and the pain that followed was hard to bear. After sharing that painful news with Kamehameha, we also shared " hā " or breath, a respected form of acknowledgment.

He told me I needed to "hemo" or discharge this painful energy and ho'oponopono for my cousin, my 'ohana and myself. This helped me release the suffocating sadness and remember the joy Justine brought to our family. It didn't erase the sorrow, but it allowed me to remember the love I felt for her. Months after seeing Kamehameha he asked me how my ho'oponopono had been going. He shared with me the energy I passed on to him when we shared each other's "ha." He told me it is my "kuleana," or responsibility, to "hemo" this energy and ho'oponopono. Since then, I have read Zero Limits by Joe Vitale and Dr. Ihaleakala Hew Len. I've been inspired to clean and clear with ho'oponopono as much as possible.

I understand ho'oponopono to be a practice of encompassing compassion with the world and all its beings. Every day, in every step we take, we create our personal memories. Each choice can create a connection to each other and our world we live in. Everything you see, everything you hear, every person you meet, you experience in your mind. I believe there is a connection to our memories and, in turn, there is an impact to ourselves. The force of what we see and what we feel comes from within.

With Dr. Ihaleakala's ho'oponopono practice, there are four simple steps to putting ho'oponopono in action in our lives and the order they are done is not that important. Repentance, forgiveness, gratitude, love and thanks are the only forces at work – and I've found them to have amazing power. The way I hope to live my life is on a path full of aloha, innovation, inspiration and reaching for goals through positivity and clear energy. But, just like you, I sometimes get stuck. Getting stuck or frustrated can be thought of as having "stuck energy." The way we think about or reflect on the many memories we have can be the reason we feel stuck.

A first step is asking for forgiveness and saying, "I'm sorry, please forgive me." You don't need to direct this toward anyone in particular, it can be yourself (or God, or the Divine, or the Universe however your belief would lead you). This process has helped me clean myself of difficult memories or stuck energy, and have faith. You then direct your energy again and say, "Thank you, I love you." It sounds silly, but for some reason it is so rewarding to feel such positivity and turn this into a form of mantra when you practice any type of meditation or prayer.

As 2017 began it coincided with a time that I had been practicing mindfulness and meditation that was influenced by ho'oponopono. Throughout the day I repeated, "I'm sorry, " "I love you," and "please forgive me." On a day in early January I wrote the following in my journal. It was a day of enlightenment.

Journal Entry for this day in January 2017

DATE 1 / 9 / 20 17

Never give up on a dream just because of the time it will take
to accomplish it. The time will pass anyway.

EARL NIGHTINGALE

I am grateful for...

1. My dreams
2. My Divine self & unconsious thought Process
3. The new book im reading, "Zero Limits" by Joe Vitale

What would make today great?

1. Getting all my things together. Finishing Packing for Oahu.
2. Calling to arrange Pick-up for my board tomorrow
3. Checking in & Spending some time w/ Grandparents.

Daily affirmations. I am...

I am divine.

Punalau PuPPy   *3 Amazing things that happened today...*

1. Practiced Ho'oponopono today & was enlightened when seeing a clear step towards a clear desired outcome
2. Went on a beautiful whale watch on Gemini on Kimi's invite
3. Got to help grandma C. Fix her fence for Max & dropped off the New Balance Shoes I got for grandmas B-day for grandpa!

How could I have made today even better?

By taking racks off my truck & starting to load my truck for dump sooner, allowing me to Fit everything into my truck & not have 164 More left out for another time!

From my January 9, 2017 Journal: At 7 am on the morning of January 9, I was perfectly comfortable while sitting in the bathtub listening to *Zero Limits* when I was interrupted by a phone call from my lifelong friend, Kawika Kinimaka. He invited me to surf Windmills. Despite plans to hang at home that day and finish packing for my flight to Oahu for the "Backdoor Shootout," I decided to take the book's advice (and my own natural instinct) and go with the flow.

I hurried to pack my surf gear in the truck so I could head to Windmills and meet Kawika. On my way there, just after I passed Honolua Bay, I spotted an abandoned dog. I had seen this dog on the side of the road in this same spot before. Perhaps it was the spot the previous owner had dropped him off and the poor dog was never picked up again. Normally I would have driven right by the dog and sighed to myself in disappointment for how irresponsible people could be to do a thing like that.

Not on this day. The dog started chasing my truck as she tends to do. Maybe my truck looks or sounds like something familiar, like from the previous owner. I thought of ho oponopono after a deep sense of compassion for that dog washed over me. I have experienced the feeling of being left behind in a strange country, of being abandoned in a place that's not familiar. It hasn't been on the level that dog has experienced, but I can relate to and feel compassion for the dog. I had a chance to clean myself of my own memories of being abandoned and other emotions I might be keeping in my heart relating to that. I began to recite, "I'm sorry, I love you, please forgive me, thank you."

It wasn't just me saying these words in a superficial way. I meant every word. I made the decision to turn around and drive back to the dog to see if I could share some love with it. By the time I got back there I couldn't see the dog anymore. Maybe she was in the bushes or long gone. Anyway, I got out of my truck and walked toward the bushes and spoke in the general direction of where I thought the dog might be. I channeled my mana, the Hawaiian term meaning energy, power, or to have influence and the power to perform in a given situation. I aimed my voice and energy toward the dog while reciting, "I'm so sorry, I love you, please forgive me." I also said it one more time focusing my energy towards the owner of the dog, not shaming that person but telling the Divine, with the owner in heart, "I'm sorry, I love you, forgive me."

After feeling a sense of "He ho'ailona paha," (that maybe it's meant to be), I continued over to Windmills to surf. I had a fun session on my longboard at the right breaking Windmills with Kawika, Kenny (Uncle Fruit Bean) and Boomer. We surfed for over an hour. On my way home, I wasn't consciously thinking of the dog or the ho'oponopono I did, but to my amazement, when I rounded the corner where that abandoned dog dwelled a car was stopped. The person was feeding her and giving her water. I couldn't help but feel so many emotions wash over me – gratitude, amazement, enlightenment. I was even baffled that this scenario was happening. Did I have something to do with making this manifestation a reality? It brings tears to my eyes and chicken skin to my body.

If the practice of ho'oponopono is new to you then the story I just shared might seem a bit far-fetched. I sincerely believe that "every step matters. "Everything we do matters, from how we act, the choices we make, all the way to how we look at the world. One of the things that helps me feel confident, successful and attract abundance into my life is something you may have heard from Wayne Dyer, "Change the way you look at things, and the things you look at change."

Dyer explains that this truth actually starts in quantum physics. I don't know much of anything about quantum physics, but on a gut level this makes sense to me. It turns out that at the tiniest subatomic level, the actual act of observing a particle changes the particle. Wayne Dyer can explain it better than I can. "The way we observe these infinitely small building blocks of life is a determining factor in what they ultimately become. If we extend this metaphor to larger and larger particles and begin to see ourselves as particles in a larger body called humanity or even larger – life itself – then it's not such a huge stretch to imagine that the way we observe the world we live in affects that world. Think of this little journey into quantum physics as a metaphor for your life. Your feelings of success and your experience of prosperity and abundance depend on your positive view of yourself, your life, and the Universe from which success and abundance come."

It's pretty easy to express gratitude when things are going well. But when things get tough from a relationship, financial stress, illness, physical challenges or other issues that come our way, appreciativeness can morph into doubt, anger, or self-pity. Whether we realize it or not at the time, each reaction becomes part of our life's memories. Daily reflections on what made our day amazing, or what we could have done to make it more amazing, are like making tiny adjustments in our "steps" along the path we want with all our heart. My grandmother Carolyn helped guide my understanding of this when reading aloud from her daily devotional book, *Around the Year with Emmet Fox.*

What can we do to re-discover our passion and purpose when upsets and challenges make gratitude seem forced or impossible? How do we remain inspired when our efforts meet roadblocks that seem to banish success and seem to cause our dreams to vanish? Brian Tracy says it like this, " Develop an attitude of gratitude, and give thanks for everything that happens to you, knowing that every step forward is a step toward achieving something bigger and better than your current situation."

My grandmother Carolyn always reminded me of this every time I would visit with her or speak to her. She used to tell me, "Sometimes, when you don't know what to do, the best thing to do is to just stay quiet and listen."

Her powerful lessons stay with me now every time I think of her. Every Step Matters. Every step matters in a life filled with growth, even the steps that might seem off your goal or aspirations.

Journal pages from The Ultimate Waterman 2017

DATE 04 / 03 / 2017

The real gift of gratitude is that the more grateful you are, the more present you become.

ROBERT HOLDEN

I am grateful for...

1. The gratitude beads that grandna Made me.
2. Itelectuality & gratitude Grandma Carolyn has intilled on me.
3. This HyperFlex Wet suit Jacket Keeping me warm

What would make today great?

1. Being in Rythm w/ to catch quality high-Scoring waves!
2. No matter what the conditions, have fun & Stand out!
3. Doing my best & being Proud of my Performance.
4. Bring home a win (or two!!) & having those beautiful Maori Trophies on my Desk!

Daily affirmations. I am...

I am fortunate.

3 Amazing things that happened today... over dinner & wine

1. Shared Some Smiles & laughs w/ Mana, Ash, Dr. Russel Coquira
2. Chuck Figued out the Medical condition name & info, Polycrd…sia Chuck
3. Got Some Fun waves & barrels in ShortBoard heat today.

How could I have made today even better?

By moving Further in & catching waves more towards other athletes. By being so up Further more reactive when reading the set I Just barely missed because of the fade, to re-Form section...

246

DATE 04 / 04 / 2017

One day, you will wake up and there won't be any more time
to do the things you've always wanted. Do it now.

PAULO COELHO

I am grateful for...

1. The Whim Hoff breathing technique to wake
2. An adventure aheat today w/ helicopter rides & SUPsurf
3. A fresh slate & a new day w/ knowledge from the Past, ~~confidence~~ mindfullness in the Present & faith in the Future! Confidence

What would make today great?

1. Winning the SUP surf divlSion today!
2. Sharing Some great laughs & smiles w/ everyone!
3. Oo Safe day for everyone on the water

Daily affirmations. I am...

I am faithful !

3 Amazing things that happened today...

1. I was totally in Rythm w/ the waves today, Won The SUPSURF!
2. Caught Some really fun long Rippable Rights, & beat Caio on my backside for one of my 1st times.
3. Sharing Some Fanominal views from the helicopter w/ the Whole crew, from the beach to the Snow!
4. Got to spent the day @ Big Bay, a desolate location!

How could I have made today even better?

By being more responsible w/ my things (etc. Glasses & iPhone) Connor Saved me twice where I left my iphone in Super Random Place....

As my stories have been collected in my journals over more than a dozen years, small steps have created my practice of living a life of aloha filled with innovation and inspiration. Like you, I only see what I look for, and I look relentlessly for innovation and inspiration. I look for ways to make each day more amazing, to see the path that could have brought me closer to my goals, and also instill inspiration in and find inspiration from the people whose path crosses with mine.

Success begins with a practice. It begins with a regular, consistent practice of mindful reflection connected to gratitude. Over the years I have discovered so many ways that life is created as a direct product of our actions, beliefs and attitudes. Over time, looking back on my daily short journal entries, it's obvious that my steps have absolutely been responsible for outcomes of all types. No matter what happens over time, gratitude is a step that makes sense of our past, brings peace for today, and creates a vision for tomorrow.

People. I wish I could tell every story about every person I have met over my lifetime. My family has always inspired me to listen and learn from people I meet. I have been encouraged to remember people who have made an impact on me. In turn, I try to make an impact on others. Over the years as I have dedicated my life to things I am passionate about and are meaningful to me. The steps toward my purpose unfold and so often doors open because of the people in my life.

People with a sense of purpose are driven, focused, committed, and lit up from the inside. They don't quit or get distracted from what they believe is the reason they're on this planet at this time. Having this sense of meaning and purpose provides energy and drive along the path life takes us. Notice the sense of purpose and passion, or lack of it, in the people who surround you. We are absolutely influenced by the people with whom we spend the most time

Like you, I hope to impact the world for the better. Even for the causes and ideals where I feel a sense of strong commitment and expertise, I know that my knowledge isn't "complete." There are always gaps, biases, limitations and prejudices, and new places to go. The people whose lives I impact along the way are so very often the very people who show up for me when I need support, help and the expertise of others.

I am grateful to my friends and family who have shown me the power of relationships, connection, and engaging with the world openly. Connecting with others and sharing our knowledge and talents might take us out of our comfort zone from time to time. But you will always be rewarded. Every step with the people who come into your life matters. Creating positive, supportive and authentic relationships are the small and consistent steps in your journey. Don't walk behind your peers as a follower, don't walk in front of them as a leader, but walk beside them as a friend.

All my life I have followed one simple piece of advice my mother gave me, and it has worked wonders in my life. When I was about seven years old she told me, "Zane, you have to take every opportunity presented to you and then run with it with all the enthusiasm you have!"

I can't tell you how many times that practicing this has turned a single opportunity into two, and then three. I have expanded on my global connections, networked, and have taken every opportunity and made the very most of it. I don't want to live life with any regrets. Every Step Matters!

One of the first times I followed this advice was when a close family friend Pietro Porcella, a windsurf pioneer from Sardegna, Italy, called them. Pietro said that my mom should take me and Matty to Kanaha Beach Park because Linda Stott was hosting a summer windsurf clinics for kids with all new child sized gear. My dad's sail sponsor, Jeff Henderson of Hot Sails Maui, had modified some adult equipment for kids our size. It was making it so much easier for kids to learn. My brother and I were mostly surfing at that time, but Mom asked us if we wanted to go.

We had all learned to windsurf with my Dad on big, heavy equipment, not the new kid-sized equipment. Although we were able to windsurf, we were not that good. Matty wasn't interested in going because Kanaha was about an hour away from where we lived, so I didn't go either. The following week our friend Pietro called again to say, "Zane needs to come to the kids windsurf clinic. Your family is windsurfing royalty. He could be the first third generation windsurfer." Then he added this, "Kai Lenny, Connor Baxter, Bernd Roediger and Baker Grant are all learning really fast."

So, my mom asked me again, this time reminding me of her advice. I thought about it for a minute, thinking that I would want to be able to keep up with my friends windsurfing and I said, "OK, let's go!" That small step changed my life – literally. I always thank Pietro Porcella whenever I see him. His kids, Nicollo and Francisco are also professional watermen that started off their careers with windsurfing and they are some of my closest friends too. Nicollo is a kiteboarding World Champion and Francisco won the WSL Big Wave Award in 2017.

So that day thirteen years ago, when I got to the beach I saw Kai, Connor, Baker, Jake Golm, Kalani Hunt and a few older kids like Nick Warmuth and Skyler Haywood all getting rigged up. As soon as I saw Skyler get on the water and sail away, then jump about 5 feet in the air, I was hooked. I wanted to be able to rip like that, too. Skyler made big impact on me. He was a few years older and was someone I could look up to. He inspired me to practice my skills and reach toward his level of excellence. And it didn't hurt that there were a few really pretty girls in our windsurf camp too. Linda Stott's daughter, Kanza Stott, Connor's sister, Ashley Baxter, Alexis Aguera, Nique Vetromile, and Paulina Pease were part of our group as well.

Linda made it really fun for us too. We had little competitions to see who could rig up the fastest, or water start the fastest. Believe it or not, some of the memories I remember most clearly were ordinary, funny little things like sand fights on the beach (which we weren't allowed to do) or "Rock the Board" where two kids would stand on the same windsurf board facing each other and rock it until the other fell off. I believe things like this, just farting around and playing, enable kids to excel quickly.

We would play follow the leader and we would all have to do whatever Linda did; like jibe, or jump, or go really fast. It was the best
summer for me too. For the first time, instead of trying to keep up
with my brother and all his friends that were five years older than I
was, I was now really having a blast with kids my own age who were
ripping, like Connor, Baker, Bernd, and Kai. We pushed each other all
summer long to improve and by the end of the summer we were all
as good as some of the pros. Before we knew it, people in the windsurf industry were taking notice of us. Kai and Bernd got sponsored
by Naish. Connor and I started windsurfing for Starboard. Hot Sails
gave me a full quiver of complete windsurf sail rigs, and we were
ready to start competing.

I was super stoked to be able to carry on my family legacy with windsurfing. My grandfather invented the sport, my grandmother started the first windsurf magazine, my father and mom were champion
windsurfers, and I can take pride in being passionate for the sport and
the windsurf community. My parents were thrilled too. As young kids,
we and our crew were accepted and the entire windsurfing community seemed to be stoked to have some kids competing. Especially ones
whose parents were so well known like ours. Connor's mom, Karen,
was a champion windsurfer and his dad, Keith, was a pioneer and
innovator in the sport.

Kai, Bernd, Connor and I had some incredible opportunities when we
were just groms. We all took those opportunities and turned them into
our lifestyle and our amazing careers for more than a decade so far. We
have been traveling the world together since then and it all started with
windsurfing. We all seized the opportunity given to us and ran with it
with enthusiasm. As new opportunities presented to us, we raced with
them too. We have all been flexible with our plans after starting off
with windsurfing. We have morphed into standup paddlers, windsurfers, kite boarders, surfers, big wave riders, foilers and watermen.

Pay attention. Whoever crosses your path does so for a reason. Every
step matters and every person matters. Sometimes the outcome is a
challenge or a frustration, a hurdle or a lesson to be learned. Other

times it's an opportunity, a chance to add innovation, inspiration and a relentless path to your dreams.

Do you have people in your life, or people you aspire to meet and know, who positively impact the world and obtain amazing results in their work? It is interesting to notice their process of obtaining these results. How they operate in life can be inspiring and uplifting. They are happy to help and support others. They seem to have an overflow of positive energy that enriches the lives of those they connect with. It's inspiring to notice their persistence in making sure "Every Step Matters." It begins to show us all how to create our journey as the goal. The journey contains the building blocks of the life we really want after all.

It's pretty tough to embrace failure as important "information" guiding us along the way. I have had so many "meandering steps along the way" to my goals throughout my career. Along the way through my "InZane" life, I am discovering that my ultimate goal is not about acquiring more World Champion titles, enhancing my reputation as a water athlete, or power. I simply need to live life to the fullest, every day.

I am seriously excited about discovering new ways to help and share with others what I have learned through my life experience. Protecting the environment and the ocean are crucial aspects of my life. Ideas, innovation and inspiration that I create or am able to collaborate on with others can bring positive solutions to our world.

Every step matters, even the ones that seem like terrible mistakes at the time. Thomas Edison looked at "mistakes" like this, "I have not failed, I've just found 10,000 ways that won't work."

Like Edison spent time going back over his mistakes and failures, we can too. But remember, Edison reflected on mistakes as a means of finding his way forward to future successes. That opportunity is available to all of us. We can learn from – and get past – our mistakes. Just as importantly, when success comes, take the time to reflect on it as well. A mantra that I observe and practice regularly is this, "Learn from the past, live in the present, and manifest your future."

On the day of some of my greatest successes I usually didn't realize how that experience connected to my past – and to my future. Going back over journal entries about some of the events and experiences most meaningful to me, I notice that they always include people who made all the difference. These relationships are a strong and constant thread in my life. The following story is powerful and bridges generations.

I first connected with Jeff Clark in 2016 when my sponsors at Cobian Footwear invited me to join them on a trip to Baja del Sur in Mexico. Jeff is a Cobian Ambassador, as well, and a world renowned big wave surfer. He's a legend. In fact, he's the original Mavericks surfer. Jeff's connection with our family goes way back. My mom tells it like this, "Jeff Clark was my friend. Way back in the early 80's, way before people surfed Mavericks, he had a surf shop called The Cowboy Surf Shop. He was one of the first people to give me a board and support me at the very beginning of my windsurfing career before I moved to Maui. It's very special to me that now my son has had the chance to have a friendship and camaraderie with Jeff."

The Cobian trip was meant to be a fishing and surfing trip filming for a reality television show with Bill Boyce called, *Destination Baja del Sur*. The crew for the trip was a great collection of men and I imagined it would be a fun trip cruising around on this 240-foot mega yacht for five days hunting surf and fish. The big boat had three smaller boats right on the back of it. Every day we filmed our surfing and fishing. It was really ironic. The waves were especially good and the fishing was terrible. It was meant to be a full-on show about fishing, with a side story about surfing. But we didn't catch much fish, just lots of really fun waves.

The full moon, which made the nights incredible, was the cause of the poor fishing. It was so bright that the fish were feeding all night, rather than in the daytime when we were fishing. While the fishing wasn't exceptional, the time I got to spend talking story with Jeff was great. We talked about his early windsurfing days and the beginning of surfing Mavericks. Back in those days they had terrible wetsuits, old school boards and no one out in support boats. It was just sort of freaky and lonely doing that long paddle out to the wave.

It was pretty unique to have that time connecting with Jeff on the Cobian Ambassador Baja trip because later that year I had a chance to go to Mavericks. During that trip, I stayed with him. Matt Becker, who's a long-time family friend and like a brother to me, is his next-door neighbor. Originally from Santa Barbara, CA, Matt moved to Half Moon Bay, CA to be closer to his passion – surfing Mavericks. Matt is one of the standouts in the lineup. He is fearless and extremely talented. Following in his father's footsteps, Matt works as a commercial fisherman when he is not surfing Mavericks. I felt honored that the three of us surfed Mavericks together.

It was pretty amazing how the trip all came together. I was only in California for a short time and this day was in between the Battle of the Paddle and another event. We were driving north from Dana Point. On the way, we met with Joe Bark, the legendary shaper of some of the original big wave California boards. He has been sponsoring me for my big wave surfboards for over two years now. His boards are incredible in big waves and have really boosted my confidence and surfing the 25-foot-plus waves. He gave us some boards to ride and we were really stoked as we made our way up the coast to Half Moon Bay to meet up with Jeff and Matt Becker.

To me, the weather and water were cold and I was freezing. But the locals thought it was warm. They were saying that it was unheard of to have water and air temperatures like that. Matt, Jeff and I got up to the parking lot early in the morning. We were walking out to the long point on the bluff toward Mavericks. It was cold and foggy and I remember thinking how eerie it was. The waves were pumping, so we raced to get our boards from the car and down to the beach.

It was an amazing experience for my first time. The waves were big, but not scary big. They were 15-18 Hawaiian, so that's a solid 30-foot face. We got really lucky. There weren't too many people out, which is good, because sometimes it can be a circus out there. Paddling out on my Joe Bark big wave surfboard with Matt and Jeff, I felt really comfortable since they're the "local boys" out there. Everything was perfect. I'll never forget the rides from that day, but best of all was the opportunity to share it with Jeff and Matt.

People, places and opportunities. They all come together when we are open in our journey. We make many choices and through them the days unfold. Our steps can be created through innovation and inspiration, or through distraction. Reflecting on the day allows awareness of the steps chosen and gratitude for the opportunity to learn, grow and create the life journey that's best. Every step matters.

Victory is when preparation meets opportunity.
Top photo: Tahiti / bottom photo: Cloudbreak Fiji.
Photo Credit: Matty Schweitzer / Mat5o Media

CHAPTER FOUR

Victory - Believe and Create

Innovation requires preparation, collaboration and a fire in the belly. Every challenge provides an opportunity to grow, learn and become even more inspired to work toward a victory. Something I have found to be true is this, "Success is when opportunity meets preparation."

For more than half my life I have had the habit of daily journal writing. It is a strong and valued habit that helps me stay grounded and focused on goals and dreams, but even more, it sharpens my mental preparation and motivates me. It might seem like a simple thing to open your journal every day with intention. Practicing mindfulness toward the day ahead and reflecting back in the evening might seemed forced at first. Taking time to really know and articulate your dreams and actions taken toward your goals is worth the effort. It provides clarity and focus.

"When you want something, all the Universe conspires in helping you to achieve it." This quote by Paulo Coelho in one of my favorite books, *The Alchemist*, has had a great influence on me. What you think about, you bring about. If you put all your focus, energy and positive thoughts toward whatever it is you want, you'd be amazed at what opportunities come knocking. Whatever it is, however it happens, if you want something badly enough it's as if everything lines up to give you whatever your heart desires. Call it fate, coincidence, beginner's luck or whatever sits best with you. When you put time and energy into something with all your heart, you will manifest it into your life.

So, let me begin with a story about manifesting something into my life. This particular story would be impossible even for me to believe if it had not been written down. In fact, the story might not even have ended the way it did *unless I had written in my journal with true conviction*. I will take you along with me to the 2016 Fiji ISA World Games. To begin, here's some background for the event. The 2016 Fiji ISA World SUP and Paddleboard Championship took place across various incredible locations in Fiji. The world-renowned wave of Cloudbreak was the site for the SUP Surfing and Technical Races, along with the start of the Distances Races. The distance races traversed 18 kilometers past the islands of Tavarua and Namotu, culminating in an epic finish at Musket Cove. The Team Relay Races were held on the west coast of Fiji's main island, Viti Levu, at Port Denarau.

It's an Olympic-style team competition that combines the disciplines of SUP Surfing, SUP Racing and Paddleboard Racing. The athletes compete for individual gold medals and the Club Waikiki-Peru ISA World Team Champion Trophy is awarded to the team that wins the gold medal.

Each team fields up to 15 athletes in the following divisions: SUP Surfing: Men (2), Women (1), SUP Technical Race: Men (2), Women (1), SUP Distance Race: Men (2), Women (1), Paddleboard Technical Race: Men (2), Women (1), Paddleboard Distance Race: Men (2), Women (1), Paddle Team Relay: (4 athletes per team)

This section is directly from my longer journal: It was November 2016 and I was Fiji bound with my brother, Matty, his wife, Elena, and their one-year-old baby girl, Sage. We flew from Maui to Oahu where we had a one-day layover before connecting to Nadi, Fiji. The Napoleons hosted us with warm aloha as they always do. I feel very blessed to have the Napoleon ohana in my life and their son Riggs Napoleon as a close friend. The Napoleons are very respected family of true watermen in Hawai'i and have a lineage of talent and connection to the ocean, from paddling the Molokai Channel to pulling into huge barrels at Makaha. Aaron Napoleon and his father, Nappy, were multi-time Molokai2Oahu champs. Riggs is following the family tradition by racking up many titles already, at just 20 years old.

I met Riggs when he was 10, I believe, and now get to know his nephews Hoku, Isaiah, Izu and Titus. Before leaving for the airport the last night of our visit, we sat around the fish that Riggs had caught off his canoe (wa a) that morning and I felt a sense of pride and gratitude for my relationship with his ohana. I was watching baby Sage looking at the aha (fish) along with Riggs and his cousins and friends. I have no doubt that the relationship among them will grow deeper as they grow and become close. It will move into another generation of our ohanas together.

I also got to connect with Paul Pastana the day we arrived which was epic. Paul has always been a close friend and it's always a pleasure to connect with my Maui Boyz. We had dinner at Wild Buffalo Wings with Matty, Elena and Sage. We talked story about how time flies and how people, including our friends, change for the right or the wrong.

As I write this I have actually just landed on Fiji after two flights from Honolulu, to Christmas Island and then Christmas Island to Fiji. We traveled with some of our Team Hawai'i representatives, including Lara Claydon, Uncle Andy Claydon, Talia Decoite, Matty, Elena and Sage. Auraii e hele kākou ho'omaka ia huaka'i

Journal Entry from November 7, 2016

Leave to Fiji

DATE 11 / 7 / 2016   ☀

Looking at things from other people's point of view
is practically the secret of success.

PAUL GRAHAM

I am grateful for...

1. Feeling Confident w/ my equipment & what im Packing
2. Feeling Healthy & clear
3. For all of the opportunities ahead of me..

What would make today great?

1. Bringing everything im going to need.
2. Being invited to stay @ Riggs' or Kamu "Sam's" house
3. Getting Sam to join Team Hawaii for Fiji!

Daily affirmations. I am...

I am going to win the ISA World
Games in Fiji & become 2016 ISA Gold Medalist!

🌙

3 Amazing things that happened today... @ Wild Buffalo Wings
1. Got to have dinner w/ Paul Pestana on Oahu!
2. Spending a brief moment w/ the Napoleons & their keiki!
3. Hearing the news from Matty that he passes Part 107 pilot
license...

How could I have made today even better?

By going on a run...

Journal Entry: Day before Final SUP Surf day - November 2016: Musket Cove Island Resort and ISA Races

This was the second year with Matty coaching the ISA championships and the first year he was doing it alone. Fiji was an expensive trip for Team Hawai'i but we rallied the funds and got the team out there thanks to the generous support of the Palladium Hotel Group, Maui Jim and Pacific Honda. As Team Hawai'i, we are best in extreme conditions. The entire event up until the last day was complete, tourist-postcard Fiji: blue skies, warm water and hot air without a breath of wind. That is not what Hawaiians are good at. We excel in big waves and windy conditions.

During the first few days of the event with the small waves, our Team Hawai'i was hurting. Matty and the Australian coach rallied up a majority of the coaches (about 26 out of the 32 teams), to suggest a change in the event schedule. There was a chance that during the last few days of the holding period Cloudbreak could get big. A schedule change would mean that the athletes would have to race their Technical and Distance Races in completely flat conditions, but it would allow us to be able to surf in some good-sized waves later on in the week.

Kai Lenny was on our team and he is one of the best down-wind racers in the world. I also excel in downwind conditions, but we knew the event would not have any wind. We put our minds to being the best we could be in the conditions. So, in completely flat conditions Kai got 7th and I made it to the finals in the sprint racing by placing 10th among the world's best.

We both made it into the finals of the Sprint Racing Technical division as well. I was really humbled and appreciative with my result since I hadn't really been training for the race portion of the Worlds. This was because Connor Baxter (the Current World Champion Racer and Team Hawai'i co-captain) was supposed to be representing our team in the racing divisions and compete alongside Kai. But Connor had an injury and had to pull out of the race at the very last moment. This meant that I was now racing since I was the Alternate Qualifier for Team Hawai'i.

Luckily, Kai had a great performance, as usual, and earned the silver medal with a 2nd place finish in the Technical Race after a monumental push from the last buoy turn to the finish. We were all so stoked as it was our first medal of the event for Team Hawai'i.

We then moved our accommodation from Bay View Cove to Musket Cove Island Resort to be closer to the next competition area. What an epic change of scenery. It was a beautiful resort and we were all happy to be much closer to the event site for the Distance Race and the Surf competition at Cloudbreak.

The Distance Race was crazy hot and continually flat without a breath of wind. Not only that, we had an up-current pushing against us. I pushed as hard as I could and was stoked to finally be able to break away from my pack in between Namotu and Tavarua Island in the strongest up current zone.

I was able to use this as an advantage since everyone else was having a harder time there. I caught the only bumps in my race in this zone and created a small gap on the second train of racers, but not enough to catch up to the lead pack. So, in completely flat conditions, somehow Kai was able to beat most of the field and finish in 7th place, while I finished in a respectable 10th place overall against the fastest racers in our sport. I was stoked because it positioned Team Hawai'i for a better overall result.

In order to jump ahead of Team USA in the ratings, my goal at the start of the race was to finish ahead of their two top racers and I did. Team USA was represented by world class athlete Giorgio Gomez, who just keeps getting better each event, and Chuck Glynn who represented Team USA the year before with their Gold Medal performance. Giorgio raced really well and ended up in 11th place and Chuck Glynn was just a few positions behind him. So, we were all celebrating.

Unfortunately, at the finish line of the race I heard that I might be disqualified because I passed the Namotu Island buoy on the right side instead of on the left. I didn't have any advantage from this, because I actually traveled further than the others, but I learned I might still be

DQ'd. There were 12 people who went the wrong way the day before and a few more today in the race, but I didn't know if they were also possibly getting disqualified. I was so bummed. I felt like I let my team down. I remember taking time alone, allowing myself to regroup after hearing the disappointing news. I was dispirited, beating myself up there on the beach, away from the others, and alone.

How could I have made such a rookie error by taking the buoy on the wrong side? There was no advantage at all! I was so completely devastated because, not only could I get DQ'd, but the Team would also lose out on the valuable points I earned. Without those points, there was no way Team Hawai'i could finish top four and on the medal podium. So much was riding on my shoulders.

Then Matty and a few other team coaches learned about the twelve prone paddlers that had rounded the mark incorrectly the day before and were still awarded medals. Matty read the rule book and it clearly said that all of those paddlers should have been disqualified. They had already been awarded their medals. This meant that if the rules were to be followed, then all those competitors would have to have their medals stripped, and new ones awarded to other athletes that finished behind them.

I just had to wait it out until the next day to hear what the final call would be. Once I was ready to return to our group, our Team Hawai'i Prone Coach and family friend, Alan Pflueger, was there for me to lift my spirits and remind me that the surf event was my real prize. As always, it's the people who make all the difference.

MY WORD: I wrote the following in my journal the day before the SUP surfing event.

I am committed to winning the 2016 Fiji ISA World Games in SUP Surfing. I will meet this by being prepared with my equipment, by being conscious and being aware of myself, my feelings and being aware of my surroundings and the environment. I will honor this by doing my best to have great wave selection and ride the waves with speed, power and flow resulting in two perfect wave scores. I am committed to being clear and honest with great commu-

nication skills. I will honor this by continuing to pursue learning languages, Hawaiian and Spanish and have an open mind to taking on new languages, including Japanese, as I already have an understanding of those languages.

I am committed to always innovate and inspire. I will honor this by always bettering myself and my abilities, and always continuing to learn from my surroundings, environment, resources and mentors. I will honor this by not just always striving to better myself, but also those around me. I am committed to share my aloha spirit daily.

I am so excited to surf tomorrow for the last day of the Sup Surf Competition! I feel great and I am stoked on my quiver of boards and all my equipment! The waves should be better than the first few days of the surfing event but, no matter what the conditions, I'm ready! Mahalo e ke akua for this opportunity for me to become World champion. This is my dream and tomorrow it will become my reality! 'Ae mai ia'u kēlā kaua.

The day of final competition, the SUP Surfing event, I felt the mana energy and knew that I had prepared myself as best I could in the days leading up to the event. Even the morning of the event I did my favorite routines – such as my "meridian stretches" designed to realign chi and energy flow.

I prepped and stickered all of my quiver of boards and paddles. By doing this the energy mana was being transferred with intention to achieve my dream, the goal which I worked hard for mentally and physically ever since my win at the 2016 Ultimate Waterman. I prepared with intention and a hyper-focus that included believing, wishing, training, and enjoying the ocean all with the intent and determination to achieve this win.

That morning on our way out it was really windy and rough. In the midst of the chaos we got the message from the Head Judge that none of the athletes (including me) would be disqualified. My 10th place overall result was now official. The entire team and I had such a huge sigh of relief after hearing the great news. Five minutes after that we heard that news we had another great thing happen to us. Two dolphins began drafting the "Thundercloud," the trimaran sailboat the

Fiji Surf Company had organized for us. The dolphins were playing and leaping over our bow. I looked at it as a great omen for Team Hawai'i and translated this sight to two Hawaiians, Mo Freitas and I, bringing home a silver and gold medal.

Now, we all needed to focus on the weather and the possibility of a really big swell coming in. The wind was building in strength, so we hoped that competition would not be postponed. But as we approached Cloudbreak after about an hour ride, we could see the white water. The waves were solid and the competition was ON! It was a really heavy event and the waves just kept getting bigger and bigger throughout the day. Cloudbreak was living up to its reputation as a world class surfing break once again.

I started off the final day of competition in the first heat, with one of the most fun heats of my life. I was getting barrel after barrel, feeling in rhythm with the right timing just as I visualized and manifested with my mindful tapping exercise on the Thundercloud that morning on the way out to Cloudbreak. The next two heats, the quarter final and the semi-final, didn't go as smoothly as I was hoping for. I barely squeezed by in second place to advance. I didn't let that get me down. I told myself I'd have a sandwich of fun heats with success the first and last heat of the day and it was just that – and MORE.

Matty was on the jet ski pretty much the entire competition which allowed him to be coaching the team throughout. He had a unique perspective and describes it like this, "The finals and the semi-finals were something I will never forget. Kai Lenny was on the ski with me and we were cheering on our teammates, Zane and Mo Freitas. We were right there on the lineup, on the jet ski, right there in the surf with them. We got to see every wave firsthand. They couldn't really hear the scores so we'd relay the scores to them as they were paddling back out. It was a really special event with two guys from Team Hawai'i in the finals. The team had a chance to do really well now. With just a few minutes left in the finals Zane was in about 3rd place and Mo was in first. Kai and I were stoked thinking, yes, Mo is going to win it and Zane is also going to have a top-four finish in the final."

Just like Matty said, Mo was on fire in the final. Mo is a close friend of mine, we surf together all over the world, and I know how talented he is. He is always a strong competitor in all divisions. For me, I started off slow and was in 3rd place out of 4 finalists for most of the heat. The finalists were South African big wave surfer Thomas King, who's always on form, the super talented Giorgio Gomez, who is a goofy-foot like me and really excels in waves that break left, like Cloudbreak, and my teammate Mo Freitas. For a second I felt stress or fear come upon me, but I shut it out immediately. I do this by being present and not thinking too much. I know I perform better when I am simply having fun and enjoying the moment.

So, I took a break and I thought to myself, "No matter what I am going to have fun. My family and friends will be proud of me and I won't give up." I looked up at the sun in that moment and said, "Mahalo e ke akua no keia lā, 'Ae mai ia'u kēlā kaua. (Thank you Lord for this day, let me fight for this)." Determination and resilience kicked in and, in that moment, I heard the announcement that I was in a combo position and needed not just one, but two near excellent scores to take the lead. The heat had less than 8 minutes remaining. That's not exactly the position you want to be in, in a surfing competition, but I didn't let this faze me. I knew there was still a chance for me to do this. Instead of being let down, this excited me and made me more motivated.

A wave came to me and I surfed it well. It was better than my other two waves so I knew it would replace one of my lower scores. Still, I knew that I still needed something much better in order to take the lead. I needed a perfect ride. When I kicked out of that wave I remember looking at my brother Matty and Kai on the jet ski. The look in their eyes said it all, they looked worried and without hope. Matty told me, "You're gonna need a perfect ride, Zane."

I looked back at them and shouted with confidence, "I can still do this," and continued to paddle as hard as I could. Adrenaline kicked in and then, with less than 3 minutes remaining, I saw that Mo was sprinting in straight at me. He was trying to sit on me, to get in my head, but my head was clear and I was ready for battle.

I knew where I had to go and Mo followed. Mo was in priority position. When we got to the top of the lineup I paddled for the first set and he did too, but I wasn't planning to ride that wave. He tried to keep me off, to get in my head. But the second he backed out I caught a glide to the right, deep toward the reef with enough speed for the quick drop in. I did a kick-out to glide around him into priority position where I needed to be!

From Matty and Kai's perspective on the jet ski, Matty saw it like this, "To me, it looked as though Zane tried to catch a wave, turned off and didn't catch it, then swung around and just somehow got momentum from that wave. He did this really fast paddle out from the back of the wave past Mo, to this perfect, big wave that was coming in. It was about 10 or so seconds until the end of the heat."

There was no way Matty or Kai could have anticipated what I saw as an opportunity. The next set, directly after the one they were seeing, was the one I wanted. The paddle battle with Mo did not stop, but I knew I had the edge of speed and was now I in priority position. I got into that wave with priority. Immediately I pulled into a nice deep barrel since we had battled each other until we were deep on the reef and in the lineup. This allowed me to start off the wave with a great barrel immediately following with a small bottom turn. I continued to slam turn after turn at least six times, hitting the lip again and again, until the wave finished and my board practically ran into the reef.

From the jet ski, Matty and Kai could only see about the first forty percent of the wave, after that only the judges could see it. Matty tells it like this, "We saw him get barreled and we saw him make some great moves, so we knew it was a good ride. We just didn't know how good. Then we heard the score – a perfect 10 points! That moved him into first place. Zane was the World Champion!"

I knew that was my last chance and I ripped it as far as the wave lasted. Then I knew I had a chance. I will always remember this moment, sitting on my upside-down board because it was so shallow on the reef, and screaming to the heavens, "Mahalo e ke, ke e ʻolu ʻolu, akua, ke olu olu. Thank you, Lord. Please, Lord, please."

I was practically breaking down with anxiousness to hear if my last two waves were enough, whether or not that last and final wave to the buzzer was enough. I sat there on the dry reef praying, thanking God for giving me the courage and strength to be resilient in the final moments. I was not giving up.

If I would have had even a slim second of doubt in myself, I wouldn't have been able to fight for priority position in the dying minutes of the heat for my last chance to make my dream a reality. I think it's amazing how all your hard work, blood, sweat, and tears can come down to a fraction of a moment and the decisions made then, in that moment of life. And that it's never over until it's over.

I couldn't hear announcements or see anyone or anything regarding results for minutes. It felt like time stood still as I floated there on my board in the lagoon inside of the reef of Cloudbreak. Until that moment I started to make my way to the edge into the channel and saw Matty and Kai smiling, cheering, standing on the jet ski with hands in the air.

"You did it! You're World Champion," my brother shouted. Kai was yelling to me excitedly, "You won! You did it."

I exploded with gratitude and excitement while sprinting to the jet ski. Standing there on the back with the ultimate support team there with me, I broke into tears of joy, feeling so grateful and blessed for accomplishing this dream come true. Then in a quick moment I felt so much compassion for my friend and teammate Mo as I looked at him in the water with the look of disappointment and loss. I told Matty to pick him up so that we could fly the flag of Hawai'i together on the jet ski and share the moment together. Mo had surfed great and I wanted to share this win with him too.

We told each other at the start of this trip that we would finish first and second, and THAT'S WHAT WE DID!

We did a victory lap on the jet ski while flying the Hawaiian flag proud. During my interview, I couldn't help but feel humbled by the support and blessing I had from my peers, 'ohana, friends and fans. I felt grateful for it all. I expressed that and am proud to share my appreciation for it all.

That night we celebrated at the closing ceremony at Denarau & Rhumba Bar and Yacht Club on the harbor with an epic United Nations on the dance floor. All the ISA competitors, ISA committee and staff were celebrating together. It was classic and epic to be laughing and dancing with everyone, with all the people included in this event from all corners of the world. We had so much fun before the sun even went down. Then Matty, Talia, Kai, Lara and I headed back to Bay View Cove where they had a firework show, fire dancing, knife dancing and an epic feast lined up for us to celebrate our victory. I decided to go to Rhumba to check on Mo, who had stayed behind. I wanted to include him in the celebration - after all, we were 1st and 2nd.

Two of the Aussie Fiji surf company employees, Ricky and Breno, drove me there and we celebrated together. The minute I walked in I was thrown on top of everyone and was crowd-surfing. It was epic and felt so good to feel the support and appreciation from my friends and competitors – and on the went the night's celebrations.

November 25, 2016: Reminiscing on the trip while on the flight home this is what I wrote in my journal: *Reading my previous writings I'm getting chills. It's amazing the power of the mind – believing in yourself and your dreams and also the effect that takes place mentally, when I write proactively. Everything I wrote I totally believed in and I was confident with what I wrote on paper and the feelings I felt as I jotted it down. I briefly thought back on it consciously during the undecided moments, like when I barely squeaked by in my qualifier and semi-final. What I wrote even came to mind during the slow start to my final. Perhaps the subconscious effect had a huge role in my performance. A mix of luck, determination and relentlessness that resulted in this win – my first true World Championship title with ISA!*

Namotu Island - Post Competition Lifeguard Duty: Uncle Scotty, the owner of one of my all-time favorite surfing destinations, Namotu Island, invited Team Hawai'i to stay with them for the remaining four days of our trip in Fiji. We have all grown up surfing Namotu and have known Uncle Scotty since we were kids. We stayed in exchange for lifeguarding and looking over their paying guests on the island. We pretty much scored a dream stay on Namotu eating epic 5-star fresh food three times a day, surfing, SUP surfing, longboard surfing, hydrofoiling, fishing and sharing good times with each other and the guests.

The best part was being there with Kai and Mo just for fun and with plenty of time to hang out and bond. Most of the time we're butting heads and really competing against each other. We always support each other because we're all from Hawai'i, but this was a whole new level of camaraderie. We all were staying in close quarters so it was really rad to be able to bond with Kai and Mo without any pressure. I've known Kai my whole life and we've always been close friends, but we are always competing against each other. This was a great opportunity for us all to be staying together in a cottage on Namotu for four days with lots of time together just hanging out as friends.

We were lifeguarding and getting great waves, connecting in a way we hadn't had a chance in recent years. In the last decade Kai and I see each other all the time, but it's usually at competitions. This trip, being part of a team together, was an entirely different dynamic. It's always fun to hang out with the top competitors in the world, especially when you take away the competition aspect.

Unfortunately, Matty, who organized for us to stay there, was not able to stay with us because of his baby, Sage. They don't allow children under age 12 on Namotu Island unless the family books the entire island. As for us, Kai, Mo and I just basically had to take guests surfing with us. Luckily, there were a few decent surfers so we were able to surf Cloudbreak quite a bit. The guests didn't last too long out there, but we had a jet ski so we could stay out longer.

We were up around 6am everyday so we got in about three sessions a day when the guests were just cruising. Two of the days were solid 6-8 feet Hawaiian, so we scored hard. One day, the wind scared off the crowd so we scored Cloudbreak just for ourselves for three hours until sunset and the conditions got really good. It was insane – barrel after barrel of solid 6 to 8-foot Cloudbreak surf just for us, for me and my teammates and friends, Mo and Kai.

On our last full day, the waves were great and Matty came over to surf with us. I was SUP surfing and having a blast. I was so happy that Matty finally got to score some epic waves and a get a change of attitude. He had been working his ass off managing the team and also stressing on the details of financially supporting the team, his family's expenses during the entire trip. And the cherry on top of it all was when he not able to stay with us on Namotu and had to stay at Bay View alone. He's such a great surfer. He needed a great day on the waves and he got it.

One of the waves I caught I saw lining up to be a sick one and down the line. Matty was there in good position as well, so I called him in on it. It turned out to be one of the best barrels of the trip. I was extremely relieved and stoked that Matty was able to have some fun and score.

Even though the surfing was epic, on our last full day Mo and I went fishing with Uncle Scotty, Uncle Victor, Uncle Neil and Fijian Uncle Joe. It was somewhat of a bonus to be enjoying a sunset cruise, sucking down some Coronas and bottom fishing. We were fishing at depths of 280-500 meters but the magic zone seemed to be 350 meters, about 1200 ft. Because of the depth we were using some rad electric reels with two big hooks and a bunch of cut up fish on them. They were rigged with some lead on the bottom and a light on the top.

Mo caught the first fish. It was a nice grouper that looked super funny because the eyes were popping out from the quick change of pressure from the deep depth to the surface. Scotty hooked an onaga (or firetail, as they call it) shortly after as the grouper was coming up. It was such a funny style of fishing since the electric reel does most of the work with just a click of a button– at the right time, of course. We would all be stoked and cheer over beers as the electric reel would reel the fish up from 350 meters, which took a few minutes.

I was up next and we tried to get back to the spot where the first two fish were caught. I hooked up one, but not easily, as the fish just nibbled on the bait. I tapped the auto reel for a few seconds to try to set the hook and play with it, then I felt it really bite so I clicked it on full. It was a fighter. As big as the pole was, it was bowing wildly with the fish's head whips. The automatic electric reel struggled a bit at times and would stop for a second when the fish really put up a fight. We just sat there drinking our beer, waiting to see color near the surface.

Uncle Scotty is a champion windsurfer and close family friend. He's also hilarious, a classic Aussie, and was giving me a hard time while I fought the fish, as he knew it was going to be a good one. We saw red and Uncle Victor Lopez was gloved up and ready to pull it in as I waited for the moment to hard reel it in the last 30 feet. It turned out to be a huge firetail or Onaga, as we call it in Hawai'i. It was definitely the biggest bottom fish I have ever caught. It was a beautiful big red fish with a long red tail. I thought about its precious life and gratitude for being able to catch it and feed the guests with it. I know how proud and jealous my dad would be. I did feel bad for a second, knowing how precious its long life had been and abruptly ended with a tug of a line. I felt especially bad knowing it was not going to feed me and my family directly.

I love to fish but also believe that all life is precious. I don't fish as a sport. When I do fish, it's rewarding when I can prepare it myself to feed my family, just like at home.

After that we trolled covering three levels: deep with a downrigger, cut wire and just under the surface with outriggers, and lines on the surface splashing in the middle. This was Thanksgiving Eve and we started to see Uncle Scotty go ADD wanting more. But we were starting to feel ready to go in and eat dinner with everyone. As the sun came close to setting we came up with a game plan to get us in. We didn't involve Scotty in the plan which was; finish all the beer, tangle up the lines, and hope that Scotty would then call it a day. It was hilarious. I don't drink much and I remember lying on the rail of the boat feeling the effect of relaxation and a number of Coronas. I was lazily leaning on the outrigger, hanging over the water, looking in at the beautiful island of Namotu. I reflected on the trip, all the good times, the humbling moments of competition, and most importantly the laughs, tears and connection we got to make with our team and the people around us.

I also wondered what it would be like to be in King Scotty's shoes, living on his beautiful but tiny island for so many years, possibly only worrying about keeping his guests happy, the weather and "making that money and riding the bull." That comment is an inside joke between Kai Lenny, Mo Freitas and me. Fishing and surfing. It's like a little heaven or piece of paradise. Even though this is my favorite place on Earth to visit, I don't think I could be content being there year-round. I am used to being a world traveler. As I leaned over the water lying on the rail and outrigger, I remember thinking, "I need more than the feeling of being content. I believe that if you're not growing, you're dying."

For me to grow I need to experience diversity, share with others, learn for others, be there for my community and be influential in doing my best to innovate and inspire and make this world a better place. Strive for excellence. I mua kekoa!

Through victory or loss, there's a driving force that keeps us digging deep.
Sapinus Tahiti.
Photo Credit: Ben Thouard

CHAPTER FIVE

Dig Deep

The stories in the "Every Step Matters" chapter set the stage for understanding the importance of how all our choices, our steps, accumulate into the life we create. Actions and their outcomes are all part of a journey that has ups and downs, currents and waves. Rather than a superhighway toward our dreams and goals, life hands us meandering paths. A path zigs and zags – it is never a straight line. The straight line pulls us toward a destination; we feel obliged to keep moving and to get somewhere. The meandering path, on the other hand, encourages us to slow down and to spend time on each curve, connecting with and learning from each bend.

It is the same with life. With each challenge or loss, we see things differently. We learn. We appreciate. We participate more fully when we reflect and become more present. "Attention drives intention." What do we pay attention to even in a loss or great disappointment?

My dad has always drilled into my head, "With every action, there's a reaction." This lesson has always stuck with me because it is so simple, yet so straight-forward and true. With every action, there is a reaction. When I have a loss, the first thing I do is think deeply about the actions or reasons that could have caused this outcome. What could I learn from or what could I have changed? I take note of it, then I move on. In a competition, the next thing I move on to after a disappointing performance or outcome is being there for the other competitors. My usual reaction is sharing aloha and embracing camaraderie with my team and competitors. I still like to make use of my valuable time, especially after a loss. It motivates me to be more involved and a part of the event.

As a competitor, I am fighting against every other competitor. So, when I am eliminated after a loss I have an unplanned, yet unique, opportunity to connect with the other athletes. Cheering for them, learning from their style on the water and supporting them creates a powerful connection. This builds an even stronger bond among us. This is good because these are the athletes I have traveled the world with for 10 months of the year, every year, for the past six years. So, after losing a competition I have to adjust my course, reset my compass and experience the new path with an open heart and mind.

I'm not saying that's always an easy transition to make. Sometimes I have to dig deep because, while I won't be a part of the experience as I had planned, I find a way to still play a role for the day. I encourage myself to learn and to be in control of my reaction. It goes back to a phrase that continues to inspire me, "Learn from your past, live in your present, manifest your future."

What you think about, you bring about. If you put all your focus, energy and really dig deep when needed along the way, you'd be amazed at what opportunities come knocking. Whatever it is, however it happens, if you want something badly enough you can manifest whatever your heart desires. Are you aware of the dream, goal or passion you want to manifest in YOUR life?

We don't just "find" our calling. Once we feel it, once we know it, we have to fight for it. People with a passion have a sort of "fire in the belly" as they relentlessly chase their calling in life. And it's worth the fight. Most of us start at the bottom, maybe more than once, in order to reach the "top" we dream of. As you read this are you dying to get up in the morning and go do your work – or do you plan for the time to follow your passion? My passion is to be in, on or under the ocean. Becoming well known for my waterman skills and to earn world championship status has been a goal for my entire life.

Like the waves that can knock you down, hold you under and work your body, mind and spirit until you're ready to break, so can an assault on your health. Of all the gifts in life, good health is usually not honored until it is lost or threatened. Anyone who has had a major health issue knows that the only way to come back is to "dig deep."

So far in my life, one of the most major obstacles I've had to overcome has been a health challenge. I became very ill, fatigued and sick after a long couple of months competing non-stop in Mexico, Bali, Brazil, Peru, Tahiti and Thailand in 2011. The condition lasted for over two years and hospitalized me over eight times during my travels in foreign countries over the period of time I was dealing with it. Not once did I get a positive diagnosis, only suggestions that I may have caught an amoeba or parasite from one of the many countries I had visited.

I was never provided a treatment that helped. Instead I was just fed antibiotics until my body started to shut down. I lost over 15 pounds of muscle and healthy weight while being terribly fatigued and nauseous most of the hours of my days. From the parasite, I was run down and from the antibiotics given to me by these doctors over a course of 8 months, I only became more sick and weak. Sometimes I would get violently ill in a way that would knock me out completely for over a week at a time.

After being seen by specialists all over the world; from the Center for Disease Control in Hawaiʻi, to California, Oregon, Texas, Mexico, France, Thailand, and Germany, I decided that Western medicine was not the answer. I was only being prescribed more and more antibiotics, not to mention spending over $12,000 in hospital bills and tests to diagnose the problem and trying to determine what specific parasite was affecting me. Holistic healing was the last resort for me, and now I look back and wonder why this seems to be the case for so many people. There are healing powers found naturally in our environment. I feel so blessed to have met Spice Prince of Island Spice Hawaiʻi who walked me through the road to recovery.

After being treated with a powerful antidote in Mexico, I think it might have killed the parasite, but sadly it also attacked my immune system. I was left weak and frail after two years of this cyclical illness. I only started to get healthy, gain my muscle weight back and attain my natural energy once more through Island Spice Hawai'i practices and support. Spice first helped to clean my system of the parasites, which amazingly declined within three months of treatment. The next challenge was healing the damage done to my body from two years of daily vomiting, gut pain, as well as the antibiotics. The antibiotics, which were taken over such a long period of time, were killing me and my innate ability to stay healthy. Spice developed a natural diet for me. The diet was designed to get me back to health and back to the top of the podium. It included a mix of herbal and other medicines found in nature. I owe so much to this friend for his aloha and true compassion for my issue and dedication to get to the source of the problem. Spice got me back to 110%. Mahalo nui loa Spice.

Struggling through all those months, years actually, really set me back. While I lost a lot of muscle mass, almost as devastating was losing my energy and confidence. The most debilitating part of this condition lasted for over two years and still, to this day, I deal with some rough days because of the damage done. The damage came from overproduction of acid through the throat and in the stomach during those two years. I learned a lot about the importance of diet, of treating my body like a temple, being very conscious of what I put in and how that is converted to energy. At the end of the day, what doesn't kill you makes you stronger.

Those years were a time I really had to dig deep. I still didn't give up on training or give up on my dreams of becoming world champion. I continued to follow the tour despite not being anywhere near 100%. I would show up to competitions and races, weak but determined. The events would start just moments after I had been vomiting or waking up, yet I'd still give it my 110 percent. I even won a few major events during this time, including my first Stand Up World Tour title in Hawai'i in 2011, the Battle of the Paddle Junior division (and fifth overall), the Turtle Bay Sprint Races for the Stand Up World Series (SUWS) in 2013 and 2014, as well the Junior World Championship title for Expression Session Windsurfing.

But I also had to pull out of a few major races just minutes before they were about to begin. One example is my second time doing the Molokai to Oahu 32-mile race. After throwing up for two days, I couldn't even stand up, but I foolishly wanted to try to start the race any way. My father, put his foot down, even after spending a week preparing the boat for the event. He forced me to forfeit my entry with a DNS (Did Not Start). I was devastated, but it was the right call. I ended up in the hospital the next day, and stayed there for three days.

Suffering through those years made me really appreciate and not take for granted those days when I could wake up naturally, not in pain. It also proved to me how much heart and mind can play a role in chasing your goals.

I learned many lessons from this. I learned the importance of being resilient. I practiced the power of kick-starting or overpowering my body and mind with love, mental strength, exercise, nutrition and passion. Who would ever imagine that a powerfully challenging situation could set the stage for a life full of winning opportunities and a path toward success and satisfaction? The choice is always there, to dig deep or give in. For me, a huge change in my outlook and attitude came with a practice of gratitude.

How did I gain the capacity to dig deep and keep my eyes on the prize I'd set for my life? It could have begun during the time I was 13 years old and had experienced a disappointing loss in a windsurfing competition in Lago De Garda, Italy. My hopes for that event were focused on achieving a performance at my best, and even the win the overall event. But that didn't happen. That humbling loss had me thinking in a downward spiral.

My "aha" moment of gratitude occurred at this competition for the "Slalom Pro Kids Worlds 2008" in Circolo Surf Torbole, Lake Garda, Italy in July 2008. I still have the 8th place finisher's ribbon from that Junior Worlds event. Fortunately, even at my young age then, I kept a journal and have the details to reflect on. I can remember this important time in my life.

I'll start with a little back story to set the stage for who I was and what was going on in my life in 2008 when I was 13 years old. I was fortunate to travel most of the time with my best friend Connor Baxter and his dad, Keith. Connor, Uncle Keith and I started our adventure by stacking a tiny Fiat rental car to the sky with windsurf slalom gear at the Munich Airport in Germany. The stack of gear was literally taller than the little car. It was awesome. We began the trip by meeting with North Sails, who sponsored Connor and me, at their headquarters in Munich. There we got to present a slideshow of our recent trips and let them know what we had in our head and hearts for the future. They gave Connor and me a traditional German outfit called a Lederhosen customized with a North Sail logo on it. Connor and I put it on then and there on stage when they presented it to us after our slideshow and we rocked it for the rest of the day.

We got to surf the famous Eisbatch river wave in the middle of the city of Munich. We were the first people to ever SUP eleven miles down the Isar river.

The SUP down the Isar became more of an adventure than we bargained for, for two reasons. First, we came across a big dam that had a steep slope letting a rush of only a few inches of water down a long chute. Second, Uncle Keith almost got sucked into a water catchment grate. That could have surely led to his death.

First the fun stuff. Uncle Keith always let us have fun and most of the time he did, too. When we came across this waterfall/slide at the dam, we were stoked to try and surf it. Although with only a few inches of water, the fins would not clear. Uncle Keith had a Leatherman knife and took the fins out so we could slide down this fifty-foot steep drop. It was epic! We wanted to do it again, but we had to keep going down the river.

Further down there was another dam type of catchment grate sucking water into the outside bend of the river. It was almost like a street gutter that you can see in every neighborhood but it was head high, big enough to suck a huge standup board up against the metal grate sideways. It was powerful enough to suck Uncle Keith in right before our eyes where he would have drowned for sure. When he first got up close to the grate it started sucking him closer, then all of a sudden, his board got sucked from under his feet and jammed sideways up against the grate. Luckily, Uncle Keith acted quick and barely grabbed onto the top of the cement grate. He was literally holding on for his life by his fingernails.

Connor and I rushed to the side of the river and ran back up to him. We helped lift him up. It was crazy seeing two scrawny 12 and 13-year-old kids pulling up a 165-pound man to safety. But that was just the beginning.

From Germany, we loaded up the mini Fiat with our windsurf and SUP gear, but we also managed to pile on top of the load of board bags the three bikes that North Sails lent us. We were on our way road tripping from Germany on the autobahn freeway to Largo De Garda, Italy, for the Junior Slalom Pro Kids Worlds.

My hopes for that event were focused on achieving a performance at my best, and even a win. There was a lot of hype about Connor and me, the Starboard "Dream Team." There was even more pressure on me as my father is an 18-time Champion. We were expected to be on top. But that didn't happen. I fell at a buoy turn, got tangled on the buoy, and got passed by half the fleet. I was just 13 years old and the disappointment had me thinking in a downward spiral.

Fortunately, I had a conversation with my grandmother Carolyn Jackson before that trip. She gave me a task, the suggestion that would become a life habit for me. She had made me a set of "gratitude beads" that she had created from stones and crystals of different colors and meanings. She told me that at any time I could hold my gratitude beads or even just think of them and be reminded of all the things I can be grateful for. She told me, "Don't just think of what you're grateful for, but feel it. Each day list seven things you're grateful for. Visualize them, if possible. Take time to really think about your "attitude of gratitude" by adding specific details."

After that competition when I felt really beaten, embarrassed and discouraged, I windsurfed out to a rock surrounded by water. I felt like crying, but I remembered what my grandmother had said. I really didn't know the impact of that action, that important step, would have on my life but I did what she had asked. I sat on that rock. Instead of just sitting there feeling bad, I began to describe in detail seven things I was grateful for.

They were just small things. The list began with being thankful for my family who supported me and allowed me to follow my dreams, for my grandmother telling me to feel gratitude every day. I felt gratitude that my host, windsurf champion Robby Naish's older brother, Randy Naish, was taking such good care of us and showing us around Lago Di Garda. I was appreciative that I was not alone, but was traveling with my best friend Connor Baxter and Uncle Keith. Looking around the lake I was thankful for the beauty all around me, and then I saw the windsurfers and felt so much pride for my grandparents, Hoyle and Diane Schweitzer, for inventing windsurfing and influencing so many people all around the world to have so much fun. Lastly, I felt thankful that I was on a path toward my goals of being a professional athlete and getting to travel all over the world while meeting so many cool people. I was 13, I had just lost a big event that I thought I could win. I had sailed to the rock feeling sad and sorry for myself, but after thinking of those seven small things to be grateful for, I realized I felt lucky. I felt happy, and I felt confident that I could do better at the next event!

Just as Carl Sandburg explains it, I found that reflecting on my days with gratitude has made all the difference, "Gratitude unlocks the fullness of life. It turns denial into acceptance, chaos into order, confusion to clarity. It can turn a meal into a feast, a house into a home, a stranger into a friend. Gratitude makes sense of our past, brings peace for today, and creates vision for tomorrow." For me, gratitude is one way of digging deep, being present and learning from loss.

Perception is everything. The gift of loss or a situation defined as "losing" is not always what it might seem at the time or on the surface. It never feels good not to win, but we can't let ourselves dwell on the loss. It's important to be aware of the details of every loss, such as what you did right. I like to always remember and reflect on the positives first. Then I note what I could have done better, or what I could have changed, or any mistakes I might have made that could have influenced the result.

You learn a powerful lesson when you can embrace loss. By looking beneath the surface, you'll realize it's the lesson of humility that keeps us humble and hungry. When we take the time to learn from loss, it can motivate us to strive for excellence and find ways to better ourselves. Losses are what teach us those important lessons, even more than wins can. You can be naturally talented and even possibly "win" easily, but without those struggles and tests of resilience you won't learn the importance of humility, sacrifice, and determination. You won't learn how to dig deep.

A win-win attitude is very important when taking on the responsibilities of an athlete. No matter what the situation is, you can always find a lesson to learn out of it.

A loss is both grounding and humbling. When you are humbled, you are forced to go back to the drawing board, look around at what happened and why, respecting both what you have done right and wrong, as well as what your competitors have done right or wrong. You can't always just learn from yourself. If you can be aware of your competitors and learn from their mistakes or advances then you will always find an open door to improvement. Learning from the past while acknowledging that the need for sacrifice and improvement has served me well.

The SUP 11 City Tour is an adventure and endurance standup paddle race that pushes paddlers to the limit both physically and mentally through five long stages through Holland in five very long days.

Covering 220km (150 miles) across the Netherlands, the 11 City Tour has become an iconic part of the racing calendar by offering a unique event that is as much a personal challenge as it is a race. In one of the earliest years of that event, Connor Baxter and I were the two youngest competitors, at age 13 and 14, to compete in the grueling race. We were racing with athletes from across Europe and all around the world. We would wind our way through the rural Dutch province of Friesland while experiencing a rollercoaster of emotions. It was as much a mental challenge as it was a physical challenge.

Our Starboard teammate and the event founder, Annemarie Reichman, had invited us to do the event. Connor and I were curious and eager to try a race that would take us through cities like Amsterdam, mostly running on narrow canals. We would be on the water anywhere from 4-8 hours a day for 5 days in a row averaging about 30 miles a day. Connor and I were racing in the Junior Division. We were doing really well, pushing each other. Eventually, after the second or third day, we were no longer right with each other.

The system was that they would mark your time and your coordinates each day so we were starting alone, paddling alone for hours on end, until it was over. On day 3 and 4 we had really challenging conditions. Those days were 6-8 hours and very brutal, often up wind and up current. At one point a group of about 5 of us went off course about 3 miles. By the time we realized it we had to fight our way back on course in those challenging conditions.

There had been same real drama back on Maui for several hours before it was clear how Connor and I had done. My mom and Connor's mom, Karen Baxter, were watching the event on the computer. Each athlete had a chip on their ankle and so they could track where we were by watching the chip on the screen. My mom tells the story like this, "I was watching their little beeper on the screen and all of a sudden I saw them go off course. I called Karen and she was screaming too. We saw that the course went one way and they were all going the other way. They went off course about 3 ½ miles. Upwind in the wrong direction. The top five went 7 miles off course. Miraculously, they all still finished in the top five at the end of the day. However long it took before they turned around Karen and I were freaking out! We tried to tell ourselves that everything would be fine, they wouldn't be lost. We imagined that the beautiful sailboat they were staying on was following them so they would be fine. It wasn't like that, but they were fine."

It was like doing Molokai to Oahu five days in a row with no break. But worse. It was a race on flat water, with no wind or waves pushing you along. To make it even more punishing, two of the days were upwind and up-swell.

It was not only physically demanding and challenging, but it was mentally challenging. I was just 14 years old. For someone like me, to be alone and paddling in a small canal about 40 feet wide with nothing but miles of green fields and thousands of sheep was a very tough challenge. And I was just talking to sheep – for six hours a day. It was crazy and funny. I had gone through all the songs on my iPod about five times over the first three days. I was just starting to get into my head and doing the work that would make me mentally tough. So, the event was a great test of endurance, of course. But I also had to dig deep and tap into my mental strength and toughness.

Fortunately, every day after the event they had massage therapists. That was something we all had to look forward to, that and eating a big dinner, sleeping and then doing it all over again the next day. At that time of the race we only had our own rhythm and our own pace. I didn't know how I was doing, but in the end, I won the Junior Division and came in fifth overall amongst all the pro men paddlers. (FYI, that was before Connor came into his height and strength, and became the Faster Paddler on Earth).

Fast forward nine years later to the Stand Up World Series (SUWS). The SUWS takes place across the globe and Japan has always been one of my favorite places to travel to. With all the fire and passion for the sport of standup paddling in the enthusiastic Japanese community, this makes the stop on the SUWS one of the most high-quality and busy events on the tour, not to mention the athletes' favorite. The food is great, the people are awesome, and the country, along with culture, is beautiful. There was no way I was going to miss this one.

I had just flown home to Maui straight from California and my family's fundraising event, Standup for The Cure (SFTC), which has (by June 2017) raised over $1,000,000 toward the fight against breast and skin cancer. I had just under four hours to unpack from that trip in California and re-pack for Japan with just enough time to make it back to the airport. Again, I traveled with my best friend and lifelong team mate Connor Baxter. We missed our original flight, so we had to fly to Oahu to catch the next flight out to Tokyo. This meant we arrived to the event site at midnight the night before race day. It was a little tight for comfort, but at least we made it. It was especially important for Connor to make it on time because he was the defending champion.

It amazes me that every event I go to, especially in the racing side of the sport, I see so much new talent coming into the game. The level of technical and speed racing is increasing with each race. In this game, you can't miss a week of training if you want to be on top of that podium. That's why there is so much dedication into the training and traveling required to participate in the many events each season. Unfortunately for me, I had missed about three weeks of SUP training after a knee injury. The injury had gotten inflamed with a bad staph which developed into a MRSA infection putting me in bed immobile and with fever and an upside-down stomach from antibiotics for over two weeks. I was nowhere close to having the ability to train the way I would have liked to coming into the beginning of this season and my favorite stop on the Stand Up World Series (SUWS).

Luckily, I have an awesome connection in the medical industry; Dr. Sandra Goines and Dr. Shawn Tierney of Pacific Healing and Wellness. They helped me team up with "A2Mcyte Corp," who sponsors me with an in-kind sponsorship that is amazing. They share the expertise from Shawn and Sandra, as well as the cost of the special procedure which consists of a precise injection of platelets and cytokines (A2M and PRP) concentrated from blood. This process helps me and many other elite athletes get back to 110% after injuries. The procedure is something similar to a stem cell operation. Although, to get back to 110% in my world, I need 2-4 weeks of hard training prior to my goal event, not to mention the 1-2 weeks rest that's required after this type of operation. I received my operation only 4 days before the start of the Victoria Cup which left me questioning if I should even travel to Japan, let alone compete. I knew that I'd definitely not get the result I would normally be familiar with and I would be way under my goal result of placing in the top five for the Stand Up World Series for SUP Racing.

What inspired me to still attend the event was my passion for spreading aloha with the next generation of keiki (children) at the 3rd annual "Nā Kama Kai" Japan non-profit kids' clinic, as well as my commitment to my supporters and peers that were booked in the InZane clinics I host.

Of course, I charged it and made it to Japan. But what I wasn't expecting was to push myself as hard as I did so soon into my recovery process. As a competitor, it's hard not to push it and fight when that horn blows off.

This next quote is from my journal, "I definitely am feeling it from Saturday's sprint races where, to my surprise, I was holding up a qualifying position without too much effort or stress where I'm injured. That lasted up until the semi-finals, where the competition then kicked up in pace. Being only one heat from the final, I pushed it and made it into the final round. But hitting that finish line I was hurting and puking my guts out. That's as you should be after giving it your all in a paddle race, but without the sharp pain from injury, of course."

Coming into that final I was feeling like I may have pushed myself a bit too hard physically, really feeling my incision points from the operation. I still was going to give it my all and fight for the last event of the competition in this sprint final though. I was proud to have made it to the final of the technical sprints alongside the world's best, especially despite everything. When the horn sounded for the start of the final I ran into the water and took one step too far off the beach, collapsing onto my board and not getting that glide off the explosion from a "Superman" start into the water. From the get go of the race it put me in the back of the pack and in this type of short sprint racing there's no room for even one mistake. In the end, my good friend "The Viking" Casper Steinfath from Denmark, won the overall event with a great and well-deserved performance. Connor Baxter was just behind in 2nd place.

Many times, in competition, in relationships, in the course of daily life, things don't turn out as we had hoped or planned for. Each day I have a chance to turn the tide on the power a disappointment or loss has on that day or the days moving forward. Reflecting at the end of the day can be as easy as answering questions like these. My loss in Japan was partly due to an infection and I was only too aware that I was not at the physical level I knew I needed to be. Why did I dig deep and decide to compete, and compete hard, anyway?

There's always a lesson and something I can take from the experience that will allow me to innovate and to learn from the outcome. "What can I learn from this?" "How will this experience help me grow?" "What seed of inspiration and opportunity have I gained from this experience?"

The sting of loss can be quickly replaced with gratitude and learning. Sometime we can find strength through reflecting on our days and acknowledge our mistakes or challenging situations with humility rather than arrogantly denying their existence. Every step matters in this life. It really does no good for our future to carry the pain and maybe even some embarrassment of yesterday's losses into tomorrow's performances.

When is a loss really a win? Every single time – if we learn how to learn from our experiences. It's also a win when we match disappointment with heartfelt and specific gratitude. For me, my inspiration comes from my grandmother Carolyn and from my ʻohana. I hope with all my heart that I can inspire you to look at loss differently. Sometimes a heavy loss turns out to be a gift, a win and an opportunity to learn and grow.

The remainder of the trip to Japan was nothing short of incredible, an absolute gift. The next day after the SUP races it was time for some fun with the kids at the Nā Kama Kai Ocean clinic. I love sharing my time and knowledge while educating them on how to safely practice ocean sports. Part of the clinic always includes passing on the values of respecting our ocean, beaches and each other. We had over 50 Japanese kids from the community join. We organized all kinds of fun workshops for them from canoe paddle, surfing, standup paddle, swimming and basic ocean safety/awareness workshops.

The kids all were loving the action and there was nothing but ear to ear smiles and laughs in the air between them and all the volunteers on the beach and in the water. Mahalo nui loa Nā Kama Kai, Duane Desoto, Yu San, and Tristan Boxford of The Waterman League for giving us the opportunity to share some aloha and good times with the kids there for the third annual Nā Kama Kai Japan event. It was great to see some familiar faces and a handful of kids from the previous years. There's no doubt some great watermen and paddlers will come out of Zushi from these groups!

After the Nā Kama Kai ocean clinic I hosted two SUP Surf and SUP Race clinics with the help of teammate and friend Tomoyasu, a.k.a "SUP Tomo." Tomo is one of the most passionate men I know in our sport. We had nice small groups to keep everything private for a quality experience, focusing mostly on paddle utilization, board control, special stroke and paddle techniques, ocean awareness/safety and equipment diversity. Everyone learned a lot and I was honored to be able to share my aloha and "mana'o" or knowledge, with the local paddle community here in Zushi. I believe that we all are ambassadors of the sport of SUP, since it is so new and fresh, and that's why I find it important and why I am passionate about teaching. The safer and more efficient we practice on the water, the more fun we can have and the better we can represent our sport and community.

As quickly as Connor and I arrived, we left. Just hours after finishing my clinics we had one last team gathering and an epic traditional style Japanese dinner before heading to the airport. Next stop was to be home on Maui to get back into shape and prepare for the rest of the season ahead.

Fear holds many of us back in life. I was a bit hesitant about heading to Japan, based on the reality of my injury and lack of physical readiness. The fear of failing, of rejection and of other's opinions can impact us heavily. We only fail ourselves by our own inaction. We've heard it many times before: The thought of something is often worse than the thing itself. It is no different than fearing failure if we go in search of our dreams. Don't underestimate your own resilience. There is always the opportunity to dig deep, learn, grow – and share your expertise and time with others. I did not make it to the podium in Japan, but there was a different way to keep my "eyes on the prize." The grins and stoke of the kids and clinic participants are key aspects of my dreams and passion.

It's funny how going back and reading a journal entry can be a reminder of all the aspects of an event. Our mind is funny and can play tricks by selectively remembering disappointments or pain. The practice of reflecting on a day is a very grounding practice. A habit of writing in the morning sets the stage for being present during the day. Reflecting on the day and writing both the amazing things that happened, as well as things that could have been done differently, delivers powerful personal insights.

Every story about my events and travel weave a blend of challenge, obstacles and awesomeness. It is definitely not a typical lifestyle. At a very young age I had to face the reality that I would have to give up everything that most kids my age did. I started traveling on the windsurfing world tour at the age of 11. My traveling only continued to grow and grow. Soon enough, for example, I would be requesting homework to take with me, then transferring to online school, then graduating early to continue my athletic endeavors. It wasn't easy watching all my friends grow closer and bond with each other, and never being there for them consistently. I feared that I'd be forgotten, but that's just teenage and high school drama. From a young age, it didn't take too much wresting the devil's advocate for me to see absolutely clearly what I wanted to do thanks to my passions and love for the ocean. That passion has always stayed consistent. Sacrifice is part of success.

When travel, training, competing and all the stress around those experiences created a chaotic lifestyle, I was able to keep one habit constant and calming - writing daily in my journal. Whether I was sleeping somewhere unfamiliar or having disrupted schedules, I maintained the routine of writing in my journal. That practice keeps me connected to the life I choose, the life that delivers me toward my dreams.

Still, the challenges remain. There are so many that have built character and performance development. One challenge hits close to heart. I am traveling internationally 8-10 months out of the year. As the years pass by it is difficult watching my family around me grow older and change. I am missing family milestones like my little niece Sage's first steps. This can be very difficult. I am feeling the desire to be there for my 'ohana, and be more involved in my home community. All the time and energy I've shared around the world with so many people from far corners of this earth, sometimes as often as every weekend, is exhausting sometimes.

There are moments when I double think the decisions I've made by sacrificing so much time and energy away from the place and people I care most about. I think about the time that will come when my 'ohana, my community, and my friends will need me, or worse, the time when it's too late for me to be there for them. And that's one of my greatest fears in this life.

In the spring of 2017 I lost my grandmother Carolyn. She had battled kidney disease for five months before she passed. It was extremely difficult for me as I prepared to leave on trips during that time. I always had the fear that it could be the last time I would see her and tell her just how much she had influenced my life. I was with my friend Pete Kosinski in Ireland competing at the Battle of the Bay when I got the news that her time on Earth was close to the end. I did everything possible to make it to her side. I arrived home late on Monday night.

She passed away, holding my hand, surrounded by her entire family, just hours after I arrived back home. She had been waiting for me and fortunately I was able to get there in time to tell her how much I loved her, and how much I had learned from her. I remember standing there with my family. We were holding hands, crying and praying over my grandmother. I looked around and felt sorrow and love, but also a strong sense of the gratitude that she had instilled in me. Gratitude that I was able to make it back to her in time.

One of the biggest indicator of true champions, in sports, in business, in life, is the ability to see adversity or difficult decisions as an opportunity, not a threat. Author Napoleon Hill once said "Every adversity, every failure, every heartache carries with it the seed of an equal or greater benefit." That seed has a greater chance of growing into something that positively impacts our life when we recognize its presence, nurture its growth, and avoid the negative mindset that seems like an easy state to fall into.

This next story connects so many of the things I just mentioned. The pain of being away from my family, friends and community is offset so much because my brother, Matty, often travels with me as my coach. In this story, it's Matty that is faced with a very adverse situation. His attitude allowed him to overcome it with courage and strength.

Going to Tahiti was always one of my favorite spots on tour. The last time the Standup World Tour went to Tahiti was in November of 2015. I won the event! We had some of the best waves we'd ever had during the history of the Standup World Tour. The wave is Sapinus, a big left-hand barrel. I remember being really proud of this World Tour victory because it was in solid big wave conditions.

Sapinus is a reef break and it is very consistent. This means the competition wasn't much of a "luck" game, it was more a game of who surfed with the most spirit of a warrior in the conditions. It was a barrel-riding game, which I love. So, the ingredients were there. It was a big wave, with big barrels, delivering so much fun.

It was a very special trip for my brother, Matty, and me, not just because of my victory. He was very involved in the win, with all of his video surveillance and coaching throughout the trip. But there was more. The day before the start of the competition we were out practicing at Sapinus. Matty was surfing with us and he caught the first wave of the set and I caught the next wave of the set. I got this big barrel and I remember kicking out and everyone in the channel was just screaming and hollering. I remember thinking, "man, I must have had a good barrel."

The people kept screaming, "Zane, Zane, Zane!"

Eventually I looked closely and they were all pointing in. I looked, and I saw my brother floating face down in the water. I turned around, paddling my seven-foot board faster than I have ever paddled in my life. I got to him, rolled him over and threw him on top of my board. By that time Kody Kerbox, another close friend of mine and a great surfer from Maui, had paddled over to assist me. We swam Matty over to the boat through the big waves pounding on the shallow reef in the full surf-life rescue position. We lifted him onto the boat on his board so we wouldn't injure him further. Four guys in the water and a few on the boat kept him balanced on the board as we got him on the boat. I was totally freaking out.

By the time they got him settled on the boat and flipped him over, his eyes were open but he wasn't moving. He was holding his arms across his chest and he was holding very still. He was worried that he had hurt his spine or his neck. We drove him straight from the boat to the hospital which was close, only 30 to 40-minute boat ride and a 20-minute taxi ride. I remember calling our parents and all I could tell them was, "Matty has had an accident and he's not moving."

It was heavy, because it was the first time we found out that Matty had epilepsy. After all the results of the tests and hours at the hospital, working to communicate from French to English, we learned that thankfully he ended up with no damage to his neck or back. He had hit his head and neck enough to trigger an epileptic attack. He had a seizure in the water, combined with the smash of his head and elbow. That's why he felt a shock throughout his whole body with the hit. He was having his first seizure and that's why he couldn't move for a while.

I also forgot to call our parents back until the next morning so they had a grueling fifteen hours of worrying. That turned out to be a really tough time for Matty. The doctors said he couldn't even take a bath, let alone surf. But over time he learned more about his condition. He changed his diet and started on a naturopathic remedy. He overcame many of the limitations of that diagnosis and I happy to say he is back on the water surfing again, many times on the biggest waves out there!

Back to Sapinus. I had been at the hospital all night with Starboard's team manager, Caren Forbes, and Matty. We got back about 2:00 a.m. I had some food and went to sleep. I had to get up at 6 a.m. to surf on the first day of competition. There were three days of competition, but I couldn't do less than my very best on that first day. It had been a really heavy 24-hours but I went into that first day strong. Somehow, I won every single heat of the competition advancing all the way to the final. I got the highest scoring wave total for the top three waves and I won overall.

Fatigue and worry for Matty could have sabotaged the way I approached the event that day, but attitude and gratitude gave me a strategy and focus on the job at hand. Matty had learned he had a serious health condition, one that was delivered by absolute surprise. We all lived through a very scary night before learning what had really happened. Anyone who has had a major health issue knows that the only way to come back is to "dig deep." Like the waves that can knock you down, hold you under and work your body, mind and spirit until you're ready to break, so can an assault on your health. Of all the gifts in life, good health is usually not honored until it is lost or threatened.

My passion is to be in, on or under the ocean. Becoming well known for my waterman skills and to earn world championship status has been a goal for my entire life. People with a passion have a sort of "fire in the belly" as they relentlessly chase their calling in life no matter what the obstacles. And it's worth the fight. Most of us start at the bottom, maybe more than once, in order to reach the "top" we dream of. Dig deep – "Learn from your past, live in your present and manifest your future."

Bursting with gratitude when my preparation met the opportunity to win the Prone Paddleboard division of Red Bull's "The Ultimate Waterman" 2016.
Photo Credit: The Ultimate Waterman / photographer Scott Sinton

CHAPTER SIX

Attitude of Gratitude

It's pretty amazing that almost everywhere you look these days there are articles and books sharing the transformative power of gratitude in a life. Long before that was such a trend, I was inspired to develop my personal "attitude of gratitude" from my 'ohana, particularly from my maternal grandmother, Carolyn Jackson. Earlier in the book I shared some stories of how that path has been impacting my life ever since.

When thinking about the stories to share in this chapter an image came to mind. You've probably seen something like it. A motivational speaker or teacher holds up a glass of water that is half full or half empty depending on how you look at it. Of course, anytime there's water in the conversation I'm reminded of the ocean. It seems my life is a glass full to the brim with the sea.

The half full glass is a great metaphor for an attitude of gratitude. That attitude is not a passive, quiet thing in a life. Being aware and acknowledging gratitude is a daily opportunity and a daily choice. When any part of the "glass" seems empty we have a chance to reflect on how we'd like it to be filled. This is a habit that's been incredibly rewarding for me. Looking around and being open to people, events and opportunities that align with how I'd like to "fill my glass" has led to adventures, a path toward my goals, dreams and passions, and to many amazing people. All that fuels gratitude. I hope you enjoy the following stories.

In thinking about what stories to share, I remembered this one that demonstrates how early in life my passion for the Hawaiian culture and the ocean had emerged. When I signed up for the Kahoʻolawe Island Reserve Commission (KIRC) internship in 8th grade I knew it was the most interesting thing I could do that connected so many things I was passionate about. During World War II, Kahoʻolawe was used as a training ground and bombing range by the Armed Forces of the United States. After decades of protests, the U.S. Navy ended live-fire training exercises on Kahoʻolawe in 1990, and the whole island was transferred to the jurisdiction of the state of Hawaiʻi in 1994. As a young boy attending King Kamehameha III school, I remember hearing stories from my dad's friends. They could look out toward Kahoʻolawe island and see clouds from the U.S Military dropping bombs on the beautiful island for "military testing." The Hawaiʻi State Legislature established the Kahoʻolawe Island Reserve to restore and to oversee the island and its surrounding waters. Today Kahoʻolawe can be used only for native Hawaiian cultural, spiritual, and subsistence purposes.

Being able to spend a week on the island that's forbidden to visit ever since I could remember, and still to this day, was something special for sure. It seemed like an amazing adventure to be able to visit the island with my friend Chanse Uyeda and to experience Kahoʻolawe from a different perspective. It was also a great opportunity for me to learn more about my culture, the ʻāina "land," and the history of Maui county (Maui, Lanaʻi, Molokaʻi and Kahoʻolawe) and Hawaiʻi. We practiced, "mālama" or ways to tend to and take care of the land. Kahoʻolawe was the mecca for ancient Hawaiians to learn celestial navigation and way-finding- skills that were most important for navigating through the islands and all over the Pacific as they traveled on voyaging canoes.

Chanse, the rest of the interns and I loaded up into the helicopter in Kahului and flew to Kahoʻolawe on our first helicopter ride. We were enthralled by the epic view of the islands and water. We landed on the west side of the island where the heliport and base camp were. We went to the old plantation style house packed with bunk beds and we put our things away, then got ready for our tour of the base camp and island. We were briefed from our KIRC guide. He explained that the reason we signed up to come here was to be a part of this Kahoʻolawe restoration program. We would be learning to lay irrigation and plant native Hawaiian plants and trees that are resilient enough to thrive in the dry and damaged land.

By the end of our first full day on Kahoʻolawe with KIRC we learned to cut, seal and lay out irrigation with PVC and drip line. We also learned to dig and plant Aʻaliʻi and Pukiawe appropriately. Most our time during that week was spent planting and setting irrigation. We took a lot of pride in learning about the land.

We also got to experience a rad tour of the island – at least the designated areas that were inspected and were clear of bomb shrapnel. We visited the navigator's chair, which was a very special place to ancient Hawaiians and future navigators of Hawaiʻi to come and observe the winds, currents in the water, channels, clouds and the stars. By studying all of those natural forces, ancient Hawaiians bettered their way-finding abilities. Their skills were diverse and constantly practiced.

Throughout my life I have had the opportunity to learn and practice so many different sports and hone my waterman skills. Just as the ancient Hawaiians continually shared knowledge and practiced their skills, so do watermen today. It's been a dream of mine to be renowned as a waterman, known as one of the best in the world. In 2017, I was honored for the second time to be invited to participate in The Ultimate Waterman competition. I had been blessed with a victory in 2016 (More on that in Chapter Two). In 2017, eight elite watermen faced off to determine who would be crowned The Ultimate Waterman for that year.

The contest was in its third year and takes place over nine days and features eight different disciplines. It's held along the rugged coast and incredible rolling plains and countryside of the Southland region of New Zealand. Joining me for the 2017 event was an incredible group of world champion water athletes from all disciplines. Connor Baxter, World Champion and fastest man in the world for Sup racing, Caio Vaz from Brazil and the 2016 Standup World Tour surfing champion, legendary big wave surfer Manoa Drollet from Tahiti, Australia's prone champion and triathlete Jackson Maynard, Team USA gold medalist Chuck Glynn, Mexico's WSL Big Wave Champion Coco Nogales and New Zealand's 2015 Ultimate Waterman Champion, Daniel Kereopa. It was a tough field of exceptional watermen and there wasn't a repeat winner in any of the eight sport disciplines until Tahiti's Manoa Drollet won the underwater strength run to go along with his barrel surfing contest victory from earlier in the week.

I had kind of a slower start than I would have liked at the event this year, in 2017. I had earned several second-place finishes, but I hadn't won a single event yet. That all changed when I was fortunate enough to win a crucial victory in the SUP Surfing discipline in some solid surf against my good friend and Standup World Tour champion Caio Vaz. This win really helped my standings because the Ultimate Waterman event scoring process combines the total points of all eight different ocean sports. Consistency counts.

I earned some valuable points for my runner-up finishes in Prone Racing, Sup Endurance, Longboard, and Underwater Swim/Run. My third-place finish in Shortboard helped as well. Even though I had won only one event, the Sup Surfing, I found myself in strong contention for defending my title as overall Waterman Champion. The final event was the Outrigger Endurance race. I learned that I needed to finish in 4th place or better to defend my title. It was an extremely tough race against some of the fastest paddlers in the world, including Australia's Jackson Maynard and Connor Baxter. I didn't give up. I fought hard and was able to finish the outrigger race in 4th place – exactly what I needed.

After the victory, I was humbled. Naturally, I credited so much of what I'd accomplished to my family. I remember saying to myself, "I hope they are all so proud, because I'm proud and super grateful to keep on carrying the torch. I'm going to hold it with humility and bring The Ultimate Waterman title back to Maui."

After the nine days competing with eight of the top watermen in the world at the 2017 Ultimate Waterman I was blown away with gratitude to be able to carry on a family legacy of sharing joy and appreciation of nature through sport. I want to share hope through working with kids. When I was a young grom I was incredibly inspired by the water athletes and people who mentored me. I want to be that guy.

When I arrive in a new place I make a point of getting to know not only the local athletes, but the people in the town. A great way of doing this is by offering InZane SUPer Grom clinics. Surfers go everywhere in the world. They take waves. They leave. I didn't want to be another one of those guys. Our presence impacts a community and anyone can imagine a way to leave a positive footprint by sharing time or talent. Luckily, I have been taught the importance of leaving a good impression on the communities I visit.

One way I do this is through free clinics for local kids, teaching them how to swim, surf or stand up paddle. The way to happily continue doing this is by sharing the Aloha.

A few years ago, I imagined I could try to set a new standard of cool. Many kids growing up think it's cool to get drunk or do drugs. They aren't living up to their potential. But I want to provide a different level of awareness and make a difference. We can be a positive influence on the kids just by spending time with them. We can help them change for the better. Water sports are the perfect way to connect. When kids catch their first wave surfing, they usually have one of the most amazing experiences with nature. They discover a new way to feel connected and present. My hope is that they remember that for the rest their life. Maybe they'll think twice before throwing trash on the beach.

Experience in the ocean creates a very different perspective and appreciation. Hawaiians believe the land and the ocean are gods. All of nature is kept close to our hearts.

I think athletes that have connections with nature can and should share this passion, it burns bright. After experiencing an InZane SUPer Grom clinic with me, hopefully the kids will look at the ocean, at the natural world, differently.

Anyone, no matter what their life path might be, can connect with each other. They can connect with a community. Connection, innovation and inspiration can begin with the sharing of stories and experience, but can grow into an idea for sharing your passion for what you do – synching up with your sport, the environment and giving back.

The almost non-stop travel that my work requires can be amazing and incredible while also being exhausting, disorienting and a crusher on routine. Being at the top of my game, as in any career, requires consistent physical and mental preparation. To stay grounded I keep a daily journal. It takes me about five minutes in the morning and five minutes at night to write, plan and reflect. That consistent life-practice every day keeps my eyes, mind and heart focused on what I want to accomplish. Reflecting at the end of the day gives me a chance to actually express my gratitude through writing.

The TheraSurf trip to Mexico in 2011 was a very special experience for me and a very pivotal moment for my sister, Shelby. That was just about the time Shelby was going through some drama in high school and was learning how to deal with anxiety. I've seen her grow from that struggle and then blossom into the amazing person she is now. I am so proud of her and the woman she has become. Like me, she discovered that the joy of volunteering and helping others always returns more than we give.

Shelby has won two Hawai'i State Championships (2015 and 2016) and won the USA National Championship for Shortboard Surfing and Women's Standup Surfing two years in a row. In spite of her competitive success, she is still more of a "soul surfer" at heart. She explains it, "The feeling of quiet and serenity, floating above the water, feeling the wind, gives me such peace of mind. There's nothing like it."

According to Shelby, "Sports, travel, and volunteering run in our family. I am grateful that my brothers have always pushed me to sail my fastest and supported me to surf my best. We all travel to compete, and everywhere we go, we give back to the local communities by doing a free Schweitzer Sports–Sports Clinic. We regularly donate boards, paddles, money, and books to the communities we visit. My family is very close and we love traveling together. I am so fortunate to realize that volunteering for others fills my heart and I get more back than I give!! Every time I volunteer at an event it is such a spiritual experience!"

It was a great experience for us to work with TheraSurf in 2011. Jimmy Gamboa and his wife, Kim, have a son with special needs which inspired them to create TheraSurf. It's an organization that takes kids with special needs surfing. They serve youth that would never have the experience otherwise. Most of these kids had never been in the water, never mind being on a surfboard. They end up having the time of their lives. The children we taught in Sayulita, Mexico did not speak our language, but communication was not needed. The look on their faces was more than words could describe. The parents of the children said that they had never seen their child so happy in their entire lives. That is exactly what we instructors absolutely love to hear. No feeling can compare to the feeling of changing a child's life.

Shelby and I were out on the water with a boy. His body was stuck in a position similar to how he would be if sitting in a wheelchair, legs bent at 90 degrees and waist bent. Even when he was lying down, his body remained in that seated position. In order to carry him safely on the board and in the water, we had to be very close with him. We had a system where Shelby helped push us in and I stayed on the board. It was so cool, he was yelling, "Yay," at the top of his lungs.

We caught some more and he kept yelling, repeating, "Fun, fun, fun!"

After surfing for quite a while we came in. We didn't know it, but the whole time we'd been in the water his parents had been there on the beach almost hysterical. As we were walking up the beach they were crying and speaking Spanish. I could barely understand them. Eventually I got the meaning of what they were saying. Until that moment on the board, in the surf, that boy had never spoken in his life.

Think about it. This boy was about 10 years old and those were his first words, 'Yay" and "fun!"

I remember Shelby was there crying with the parents. We were all sitting around the boy. He was so happy with this huge smile on his face.

It is amazing that being immersed in the ocean will allow your natural instincts to take over. With sports in nature, like surfing, people really experience that feeling. That's why groups like TheraSurf and Mauli Ola Foundation are around. It's because surfing has been proven to be therapeutic for people with various disabilities; like multiple sclerosis, cystic fibrosis, autism, and down syndrome. The ocean truly is the world's largest crystal. When we surf, we immerse ourselves in it.

It's been proven that after 20 minutes of connecting ourselves with a grounded source, like putting our feet in wet sand or wet grass, the water actually starts to pull the positive ions out of our body and charge us with negative ions. We're so over powered with positive ions with technology and our lifestyle that we need the grounding potential of nature more now than ever.

Nature is so much a part of our being that it's the only way for us to ground ourselves. The only way for us to connect and realign ourselves for the chaos of the day is to spend time immersed in nature. The ocean is always there for your refuge and for peace of mind to ground yourself. In the midst of danger and chaos, the ocean remains the place I want to be.

Here's an example from a crazy session out at Pe'ahi, aka Jaws on Maui's North Shore. It was one of those days that was really crowded. In fact, it's remembered as one of the most crowded days in Jaws history. It was projected to be a huge swell, so many people came to watch and surf. Then it ended up not being as huge as expected. Don't get me wrong, it was still really big but it wasn't massive. For that reason, more people were in the water than usual.

I was catching a lot of really fun waves. I was wearing an early prototype of the Patagonia inflation vest. Normally I don't pull the inflation too much, I try to only use it for emergencies. In this case, however, I might have been a little more reckless than normal because I really wanted to put the inflation vest to the test. My mom, Shawneen, tells the story with this comment, "He was more reckless than normal, at Jaws, with thirty-foot waves," then she rolls her eyes as she shares that comment. I may be the cause of gray hair on both her and my dad.

There were a few sets that rolled in and I was in the good position for the wave going right. But then I looked over my left shoulder and it looked like the wave was forming a barrel going left too. At the last minute, I decided to go left anticipating a big barrel. I started going down the face. I'd gone about thirty feet down the face and was still dropping. When I got to the bottom of the wave I realized I was too far behind it. I used the speed I had from the drop to straighten out, just before the wave slammed down right behind me with all its force and power.

I made it initially when the wave landed practically on the tail of my board, but when the whitewash caught up to me I just got swallowed and then thrown all over. Then I was submerged by the crushing whitewater and I was held down for what felt like a long time. There were so many people in the way and getting pounded as well. It had been one of those big waves we'd call a "clean-up set" that came in from the outside and would catch most the people in the lineup sweeping them all in against the rocks on the inside. I remember, before I even fell, I was already trying to avoid the other surfers who got caught on the set just before. When I finally came to the surface I saw people all around me with these 10, 11 and 12-foot heavy boards. I was thinking, "Oh my gosh, these boards and these other surfers are more dangerous than these waves coming."

I was just trying to position myself out of line of the crowd and the boards before another big set wave came in again. There were jet skis buzzing all over the place doing rescue pickups. My brother was out on the jet ski frantically looking for me, but I knew it was too dangerous for him to come for me. Little did I know that he and my dad, who was on our boat in the channel with a couple of photographers, never saw me in the whitewater. My dad tells it like this, "I yelled to Matty and to the people in the other boats around me, 'Have you seen Zane? Did Zane come up?' Radios were buzzing back and forth with the question, 'Has anyone seen Zane?' and no one had. We all had a tight knot in our chest worrying that he might have drowned."

Meanwhile, since I had gone left I had a long swim to get into the channel. That swim is why most people at Jaws surf the right. It is a relatively easy paddle back to safety if you go right. But I was in an area where the current tends to pull you toward the rocks. When you go left you end up going against the current so you get pounded twice as long. It was a battle to make it all the way up and finally reach the channel through the chaos and power of the whitewater. After a long struggle, I made it across and swam out into the channel.

I knew Matty, my dad and the support crews were all probably worried but I didn't have the spectator perspective at the time. My mom tells it like this, "They were all out on the water, Matty was on the jet ski, the film crew was out on the water and Zane's dad was on the boat in the channel. All eyes were scanning the water looking for him and nobody could find Zane. All we saw was that he dropped in on one of the biggest, most gnarly lefts and nobody could find him. He didn't pop up. We were all so scared. So, when Matt finally saw him pop up and paddle around, they were all choked up because they had feared he had almost died after being held under for so long. My husband was fighting back tears. Remember, Matt has also surfed these waves many times and he knew their power.

When Zane finally got to the boat they were all ready to pull him in, to rescue him. As he got closer and closer to the boat, his dad, Matt, realized, 'He's got a huge smile on his face. He's like the Cheshire cat that just caught the mouse.' Zane paddled up to them and all he said was, 'Get me another cartridge for my flotation vest.' He wanted to go right back out and catch more waves."

I don't know why they were surprised that I wanted to go back out. I wasn't crushed or beaten from the experience. The ocean, the waves – they exhilarate and energize me. Big wave surfing has taught me the importance of staying grounded even in the chaos. I am grounded even in the chaos. Enough people got a picture from that day that I was nominated for the "Big Wave Award." I was simply doing what I do best in the ocean that is both my playground and my home.

It's worth saying this again, "Nature is so much a part of our lives that it's the only way for us to ground ourselves. The only way for us to connect and realign ourselves for the chaos of the day. The ocean's always there for your refuge and for peace of mind." Between the ocean, my family and the incredible people who have inspired me over the years, my "attitude of gratitude" has been nurtured and strengthened.

Top: InZane Super Grom Clinics on Maui. Provide for the present and prepare for the future.
Photo Credit: Matty Schweitzer

Bottom: Pictured from left to right front row: Zane, Zoltan Poulson, Sloane Jucker, Juliette Jucker, Xandri Poulson, and Matty Schweitzer.

Back Row, Seth Jucker, Shelby Schweitzer, and Ava Heller at the steering wheel.
Photo Credit: Elena Schweitzer

CHAPTER SEVEN

Aloha

A busy life is pretty common. We've all got the "have-to-do" things every day. For me, my days are full of training, practicing in the water, enjoying time in the ocean with friends, preparing for events, fulfilling responsibilities of life, travel and the competitions themselves. It's a blessing when the love-to-do things that make our life the best journey possible align with the have-to-do things. I have been blessed with the opportunity and the ability to excel as a waterman. It's both a humbling and an empowering gift.

There are aspects of the job, whatever our career, that just aren't inspiring. We might be frustrated, impatient or faced with challenges that seem overwhelming. I'm grateful to practice a daily habit that allows me to take the time at the end of each day to reflect on the day. By being watchful and observant, to being open to inspiration and gratitude on what you have chosen as your life path, delivers some surprising and amazing rewards.

Discovering a way to be and act in alignment with your passion and true purpose in life is a choice available to us all. Be observant and open. Even the small sparks that can fire you up will make a huge difference when you take the time to recognize them.

In early 2017, I was so honored to be invited by Mike Long and Starboard to go to the Maldives, for Parley for the Oceans - Ocean School. It was a super epic trip. It was just before the Maui Shootout for the APP World Tour for standup paddle racing. It was such short notice and the trip began on the same day as the World Series event. That was the one world series event in my backyard. It was the first year the Ho'okipa event was replacing the one at Turtle Bay on Oahu. This was also the only racing event in Hawai'i. It was especially meaningful to me to be there because I got second in the event in 2016.

For all those reasons, it wasn't that easy for me to make the decision to go on this trip to the Maldives in spite of all the great reasons to do so. I had been fighting for and training for the APP World Tour all year. I decided to call my mentor, Svein Rasmussen at Starboard, to get his advice and thoughts on whether I should go to the Ocean School or stay on Maui for the World Series. I told him how honored I was to have been invited, but torn because it was on the same day as the Standup World Series Shootout. Svein quickly replied, "Zane, Tikis on the podium are great. But we don't need another 'tiki on the podium' this time. You go save the world."

That's why I admire Svein so much. He truly cares about his team and the world. His advice was exactly in line with the way Svein dedicates his life and the mission of Starboard. The manufacturing process of surfboards uses many products that can negatively impact the environment. Some materials can even be toxic and create a large carbon footprint. Svein gained an enlightenment that inspired him to change things at Starboard. He realized that he had the largest board production company in the world, for not only windsurf but also for standup paddle. He became aware that his personal carbon footprint on this Earth was larger than he wanted.

Svein was determined to make that right. He made the decision to make use of alternative resources and more eco-friendly development. By teaming up with Parley and Sustainable Surf he was able to make some dramatic changes that benefit the environment. Starboard lowered their carbon footprint by 30% after working with them, but that isn't enough for Svein. Starboard was the first company to eliminate all plastic in their packaging. They remodeled their entire power structure with solar panels and windmills. But Svein is not stopping there, he plans to continue to go above and beyond.

One aspect of this goal is his initiative, the "Mangrove Campaign." For every single Starboard product sold, one mangrove tree is planted. Starboard even tracks how many miles each of the Starboard team-riders fly, to calculate and neutralize that impact. In the life expectancy of one mangrove a ton of carbon dioxide is removed.

Link: continentseven.com/interview-svein-rasmussen-starboard-joins-sustainable-surf-ecoboard-project

Svein is relentless in pursuing the solutions that work better. Not just what works, but what works better. He is a leader in eco-innovation. He seeks more than solutions that work, are efficient and affordable. Most importantly, he shares his findings with the entire world. Rather than sitting back with an upper hand in being a leading eco brand, Svein invites other companies to join in and increase the momentum of being responsible. He is amazing and I really look up to him.

Svein and Starboard have always been so supportive of what I am passionate about, this year especially. Maybe it is because I have been more willing to share what personal endeavors I want to take on. I am a water athlete to the core. Some of these endeavors could mean I participate in fewer competitions, but I may host more clinics or participate in more trips like Parley for the Oceans. I may be investing my time and energy more toward projects that I believe in, projects that *innovate and inspire* me while helping the environment.

After my conversation with Svein, I called back Mike Long who had invited me on the trip to the Maldives. The conversation was pretty funny because he was still trying to convince me to come. He said that we'd be doing a "this is living" theme, filming a Corona commercial, living on a mega yacht and there will be supermodels on the trip too. "Whoa, okay, stop," I told him. I let him know that I was calling to say yes, I want to come. The supermodels were just the icing on the cake.

So, I accepted the invitation to participate in the amazing opportunity to learn from some of the world's most enthusiastic ocean-goers. The group along on the trip included 40-50 people from a wide variety of demographics. From marine biologists, to bathymetry specialists studying the reefs and the ocean bottom, to environmental scientists, environmental activists and community influencers from actors, musicians, models and watermen, like me, it was a gathering of influencers. Our mission was to learn from each other. This entire concept was created by an amazing man, Cyrill Gutsch.

Cyrill, a German-born New Yorker, Founder of Parley for the Oceans, learned about the threat that ocean plastic poses to sea life from environmentalist and founder of Sea Shepherd, Paul Watson in 2012. Gutsch converted his agency from a design company to an environmental organization "pretty much overnight." Now his Parley for the Oceans initiative aims to encourage other creatives to repurpose ocean waste and come up with alternatives to plastic.

"We need to reinvent plastic. Plastic is a design flaw," Gutsch explains. "We have to redesign the material, and question some of the product categories. We want to invent our way out of this."

He's doing some amazing things to make that happen. Cyrill is like a vortex collaboration machine. He seems to just suck in these collaborators and influencers. For this trip, the Parley team decided that we all were the top fifty influencers in our demographic. So, we had people like actor Diego Luna (Star Wars), Chris Hemsworth (Marvel Comics superhero, Thor), and Victoria Secret and Miss Dior supermodels. On the other end of the spectrum was Sylvia Earle, American oceanographer and explorer known for her research on marine algae, along with her books and documentaries designed to raise awareness of the threats that overfishing and pollution pose to the world's oceans. Also participating was Captain Paul Watson from Sea Shepherd, a founder of GreenPeace and a pirate fighting on the good side.

There were two athletes selected from the water sports world, Greg Long and myself. Growing up, Greg Long is someone I have looked up to my entire life. I was super honored to be selected. What an honor to have a chance to learn from someone like Sylvia Earle and then have the experience of surfing and scuba diving with Greg Long, Chris Hemsworth and Diego Luna, all while being a part of something that will help us all take positive and informed steps toward eco-innovation.

The trip was so relaxing and stress-free, very different from my usual traveling to compete. I was able to pursue things I usually wouldn't have, expanding my horizons in the ocean and my knowledge around it. Every day we did presentations on the boat or at random atolls or islands in the Maldives. In between all that we were scuba diving, surfing, doing beach cleanups and getting involved with the communities of each island. We gave clinics and taught the kids to swim then we'd come back to this incredible yacht each day.

I was bunking with Kahi Paccarro, founder of Sustainable Coastlines Hawai'i (sustainablecoastlineshawaii.org). He's one of the most influential people collecting high density ocean plastic. Sustainable Coastlines Hawai'i was born out of their desire to eliminate thousands of pounds of marine debris entering the landfill or H-Power. Sustainable Coastlines Hawai'i has initiated the world's first Ocean Plastics Program.

The company Method Home has turned ocean trash into soap bottles that line the shelves of Whole Foods across the country. Sustainable Coastlines Hawai'i has collaborated with Method Home and has added collaborations with Parley for the Oceans and Adidas. His foundation supplies most of the plastic for the Adidas shoe. One night he gave an incredible and inspiring presentation on his work and vision.

Another time Sylvia Earle gave a presentation on her lifetime of work. She earned universal respect from the scientific community and made it possible for women to remain at the forefront of the ocean exploration movement. She has had more than 60 underwater expeditions, logging more than 7,000 hours beneath the surface. She is often called, "Her Deepness," rather than "Her Highness." Sylvia has set, and continues to set, a standard for male and female scientists across the world. Parley is honored to have Dr. Sylvia Earle as their Chief Science Officer. I was honored to have the opportunity to experience her presentation and learn.

We all learned from each other, sharing our passions. Meanwhile, I was one of the last to present and I was stressing a bit. What was I going to talk about? What could I teach this amazing group of world renowned influencers.

I was so humbled to be surrounded by all of these people. Normally at an event I am one of the top athletes, the one that people know and want to hang with. On this trip I was, by far, one of the most low-key invites. Yet everyone was humble. I was sitting next to Dave Hakkens, a twenty-year-old who founded Precious Plastics. He created a low-cost machine that takes plastics from beach cleanups or recycling bins. The machine grinds the plastic into pellets and then melts it into a paste-material that can be used to create new objects from molds. That is exactly the sort of invention-innovation that Parley for the Oceans strives to nurture. (davehakkens.nl/preciousplastic/the-story-behind-precious-plastic).

The experience felt like a college for ocean-enthusiasts. It was a full immersion of classes and presentations, just not taking place in classrooms. We were on a yacht over-looking crystal clear blue water with thousands of islands scattered around us. It was absolutely a trip of a lifetime. It fed the craving for education that I have had ever since leaving school. I got to exercise my mind in a way to not only to learn more about the ocean and these different people and their areas of expertise, but also to expand my horizons in the water.

I've been to over 50 countries and to some of the most extraordinary beaches and surf spots in the world. But nothing compared to the Maldives. Even from the boat at night, dancing under the stars, the sky was like nothing I'd ever seen. Down in the black nighttime water the dinoflagellates were flashing everywhere, sparkling like diamonds. The marine life was incredible, the most active I have ever seen. I didn't expect there to be so much life in an area of water in the middle of the Indian Ocean.

I learned so much about the body language and ways of communication of different ocean animals, like sharks and seals. Now I look at the ocean with different eyes, feeling more confident in the environment around me, in the currents, in the reefs, in murky water or when sharks are around.

We did a lot of scuba diving. With these scuba trips, we almost spent more time under the water with the ocean activities than we did above the water. This is the first time I ever did a trip and spent more time under the water than above the water. Those hours let me connect with the ocean and the sea life in a different way, *beneath the surface.*

Knowing the body language of various sea life, how they are moving through the water and what that translates to, really enhance my understanding of marine life. This changed my perception of sharks, in particular. We even got to swim with tiger sharks, with confidence. Greg and I were on our way to the surf session where we would teach Miss Dior, Victoria Secret models, Juana Burga, Maryna Linchuck and musician M.I.A. how to surf. We were heading to the surf session and we saw all this action in the water. We thought it was dolphins but it turned out to be sharks. So, Greg and I said, "Let's go dive."

We put on the masks and checked it out for it a bit to feel the vibe then we went back to the boat and we told the girls, "If you are ever going to have a chance to dive with sharks, this is the time."

So, we ended up taking them all to swim with the sharks. This was the first time I ever had the opportunity to intentionally swim with sharks. Surfers by nature tend to avoid sharks at all times. But just two days before we had a full day learning about sharks. We had come away with an understanding of how sharks are so misunderstood. Because of that, we approached the situation with different eyes and a different perspective. It was an amazing opportunity to dive with these sharks and to, not for even one second, to feel nervous about it. Part of the magic of that experience was to be sharing it with great people.

Afterward we all got back on the boat and we cracked open a Corona. We had ear to ear smiles, it was surreal. We were all exclaiming, "Did that really just happen? We were diving with eight tiger sharks." It was so fun and an exciting surprise to our surf mission. After that we continued with our plan and got to surf some perfect waves at the local surf spot. It could not have been more perfect.

Another great aspect of the trip was getting to spend time with Greg Long, a life-long hero of mine. Not just for his endeavors in surfing but because he's a humble man and truly genuine and passionate about what he does. He stays true to it. He also shares a lot of what he has learned, his experiences, through public speaking.

I was pretty nervous about giving my presentation after seeing and hearing from so many experts and leaders in their area of work. My presentation was one of the last of the trip. This was another time when one of the phrases I live by rang true again, "Success is when preparation meets opportunity."

The day before I was invited on the trip I had just finished a PowerPoint that I am now using in the "Sharing Aloha Around the World" school program I host with young students. It shows the joy you can receive and share from the ocean and it explains my favorite meaning of "aloha" and the "Aloha spirit" while connecting the benefits we gain from nature to our desired responsibility to take care of our environment and nature around us. My brother and I had also only recently completed the short documentary Deep Blue Life we did as a project with Sustainable Surf and Starboard. Fortunately, I only needed to change the title, adjust a few slides and my presentation was complete. It's worth saying again, "Success is when preparation meets opportunity."

The whole point of my trip to the Maldives was collaboration, sharing expertise and perspective. It was about connecting with others whose expertise might be from a niche we knew little about. The purpose was also to provide the collaborators with the tools and resources necessary to further inspire their networks to make changes for the betterment of the world. And so, my first task after the trip was to talk to every one of my sponsors.

I made a list of how I imagined they might re-design and deliver a product that was more eco-responsible. I suggested that they examine their packaging processes and explore using materials that were more eco-innovative. My suggestions were paired with my commitment to only work with those companies that were willing to take steps toward change. Every step matters. Hopefully these small steps are infectious. Our job, as part of this Parley for the Oceans conference, is to go back and influence our communities and networks.

Think about it. I have become enlightened and inspired from the experience and will be reaching out to my network, just as M.I.A., a British rapper, singer-songwriter, record producer, director, visual artist, activist, photographer, fashion designer and model is reaching out to influence her network. Our networks usually would have little in common, but the mission of Parley now ties us together. I am now even more committed to helping others see how I make daily choices that lead toward a more eco-friendly life. My hope is that they can find examples to adopt into their lifestyle. I can begin with making small steps toward habit change and sharing small actions that can allow anyone to live a more "deep blue life."

I ask myself, "How can I help more?" I want to live life as an advocate. I came away from this experience with a set of goals. These goals provide a roadmap toward actions that are very meaningful to me. The best way to make an intention real is through action and that's exactly what I am doing. For example, I share the "Pocket of Plastic Challenge" wherever I go. By inspiring people to pick up a piece of plastic if it come in their path during their surf or paddle, take a photo of it and then share on social media challenging their friends to do the same, we can demonstrate the impact of a small habit to awareness and positive action. Another example is the "#GoTopless" campaign where we promote the action of going topless and straw-less when ordering a beverage in a restaurant. We also give out reusable drink containers instead of plastic bottles to the kids attending my InZane SUPer Grom clinics. These are simple changes that change awareness and impact change for the better.

Journal pages of Goals after Parley for the Oceans Ocean School June 2017

• I will honor this by continuing to feed the Responsibility I have to protect my enviroment, Play ground, & Place of refuge - The oceans & lands.
• I will honor this by continuing to learn how I myself can eco-innovate my lifestyle & day to day habbits & actions routines! I'll Share these positive impacts & benefits these eco-innovative routines & adaptations have brought to my life, With hopes I can inspire my friends & Family & Fans to also take Steps towards a deep blue life!!)

• I will honor this by making "Pono" decisions in my Schedule, career/buisness, Personal & Proffessional life which all benefit the Well being of Mother Nature & our oceans / enviroment... Reaffiming My love for My god Mother Nature, & Commitment as an Ocean guardian!
• I will honor this by continuing to Innovate & Insire! - Leading Charge in pushing limits of our sport w/ innovation achieving 2017 ISA SUP SurF World Title - Further inspiring

A sculptor has to be a practical person. He can't just be a dreamer.
He has to be a workman, somebody with his feet on the ground.

— Henry Moore, sculptor

The gift of motivation begins with inspiration. It might seem strange that my stories about motivation in my life are connected to a word that flies off the tongue of almost everyone who lives in or visits Hawaiʻi. The word is "Aloha."

Aloha is used in both greetings and farewells as well as for expressing love. But the word means even more, it is a way of life. I have found inspiration and a strong commitment to learning more about my Hawaiian culture and language as I share the meaning of ʻAloha" with students in my school program entitled, "Sharing Aloha Around the World."

Meaning of Aloha

Besides common meanings, the word Aloha holds in itself all we need to know to interact rightfully in the natural world. These insights describe an attitude or way of life sometimes called "The Aloha Spirit" or "The Way of Aloha."

The spirit of Aloha was an important lesson taught to the children in the past because it was about the world they were a part of daily. Today's young people, and adults as well, are more disconnected from the natural world. For children in Hawaiʻi, even a connection to the ocean is not guaranteed. When I share my SUPer Grom clinics and school programs, I do my small part to keep the connection alive for the youngest generation.

I can see that the way I share my love for the ocean and our environment makes an impression on the kids. That impression is obvious from their energy and connection with me. I am energized and inspired by them at every clinic and school program. Sometimes I hear from the families. The following came to me to my mom from Jacy Simpson-Kane. The Kane's are a family that I really care about and their son, Ty, is one of our most accomplished InZane SUPer Groms. Just reading Jacy's letter make me feel I am on the right path.

"Zane has been such a big part of our son's pursuit to become a Waterman. From a young age Zane was someone our son idolized and was one of the first most influential and inspirational waterman in

Ty's life. He has always been there for our Ty, encouraging him to pursue his passions and never limit his dreams. His endless support, encouragement in all the things Ty does, and staying true to his word is beyond admirable and honorable. Ty knows that when his Uncle Zane says, 'Hey let's go surf, (or foil, or sup or train),' they are going to do it. Zane has always been someone that Ty can count on. We are beyond blessed to have him in our son's life. We cannot thank Zane, Matty and the Schweitzer 'ohana for all the continued love, support and friendship they have given our son and our family over the years.

When Ty decided that he wanted to compete seriously in SUP surfing, Zane and his 'ohana gave our family endless support, helped us out with boards, paddles and coaching. Because of all of their love and continued support, our son became the NSSA Hawai'i Regional Champion and went on to compete and win the National Title in California.

Zane lives Aloha. It›s not something that he just says. It really is something that he lives. His genuine love for the ocean and children really shines through at this InZane SUPer Grom clinics. The stoke that he brings is truly amazing to see. Many of these children might not otherwise get to experience water sports. The Starboard Starship and tandem rides with Zane are definitely our kids' favorite things to do at the clinics. Zane is sincere, genuine, kind, humble, a great teacher and leader—an amazing human. He embraces his culture and the culture of Hawai'i and every place that he travels to.

Zane, congratulations on all of your newest life accomplishment. This book, just like yourself, is going to be an inspiration to the world. Keep doing what you do. You have a beautiful heart and you will touch so many lives with this and spread your aloha to so many more."

I am humbled by the words from Auntie Jacy. Mahalo. Aloha is being a part of all, and all being a part of me. When there is pain - it is my pain. When there is joy – it is also mine. I respect all that is as being part of the Creator and part of me. I will not willfully harm anyone or anything. When food is needed I will take only what I need and explain why it is being taken. The earth, the sky, and the sea are mine to care for, to cherish and to protect. This is Hawaiian – this is Aloha!

I have had the gift of observing the power of Aloha among the people I respect most, my ʻohana, my mentors and leaders. I have the opportunity to be inspired by all that have provided their aloha to me. In turn, it is my kuleana (responsibility) to do the same.

At my InZane SUPer Grom clinics, the spirit of aloha and the way I tie in a connection to nature and the importance of taking care of the environment is as important to the kids as the water sports. An important goal of the clinics is to inspire and reach the kids while making them aware of their "kuleana." By experiencing the ocean and the land in a new way, together, they gain an awareness of how small choices and actions they make can be the solution.

Inspiration and motivation are not a one-way street. For anyone who's ever taught a child an important concept or skill, it's no surprise to learn how much the teacher gains from the experience. The kids that participate in my InZane SUPer Grom clinics always inspire and motivate me.

Can you seek out more ways to practice what really moves you, what energizes you to the core? Aloha holds in itself all we need to know to interact rightfully in the natural world. Add aloha to your personal passion, motivation and innovation and watch the fire in your belly grow. Ferdinand Foch is known to say, "The most powerful weapon on earth is the human soul on fire." What sets YOUR soul on fire?

I want to live life with aloha, as an advocate for what I am passionate about. Experiences can provide us with a set of goals. These goals provide a roadmap toward actions that are usually extremely meaningful. The best way to make an intention real is through action. Every step, no matter how small, matters.

Aloha!

Top photo: Connor Baxter, Sean Poynter and I after Team Starboard won the Manufac-turers trophy at the Pacific Paddle Games.

Bottom left photo: Connor, me and Brennan Rose.

Bottom right photo: Mo Freitas, me, and Kai Lenny at the ISA Worlds in Fiji.
Top: Photo Credit: Georgia Schofield. Bottom: Photo Credit: Matty Schweitzer / Mat5o Media

CHAPTER EIGHT

Responsibility, Pride and Humility

What is your personal sense of responsibility? What is the vision or life goal that inspires you to say, "I accept my responsibilities and reason for being, and I will be held accountable."

In Hawaiian, this sense of "responsibility" is called kuleana. The word kuleana refers to a reciprocal relationship between the person who is responsible, and the thing or individual for which they are responsible.

For example, Hawaiians have a kuleana to our land: to care for it and to respect it, and in return, our land has the kuleana to feed, shelter, and clothe us. Through this relationship we maintain balance within society and with our natural environment.

Kuleana is the active expression of the most core values in every choice we make and in every action we take. Taking care of the natural environment is extremely important to me. I have had the opportunity to work with and learn from people who are very passionate about things we can do for the ocean. I believe that I gravitate toward these people because we all feel a huge responsibility to take care of what is the source of so much joy. The choices I've made to be open and connect with the energy and passion of like-minded others truly "fills my glass" with both opportunities and gratitude. My kuleana has allowed me to live my life greatly, but not pridefully.

One of the most amazing parts of being a professional water athlete is the incredible diversity of the places I visit and people I meet. I believe that part of being an elite athlete enjoying the natural resources that are the ocean, rivers or lakes is to respect and appreciate those gifts. In my mind, I believe that we are responsible for being ambassadors of our sport and our homeland. It's part of the attitude of gratitude I have for the life that has been given to me.

Here is an example of a very fortunate meeting, one that took place in exactly the same way that many great friendships begin - on a surf trip. During an R&D surf trip to Starboard headquarters in Thailand it happened that Michael Stewart, one of the founders of Sustainable Surf, and I were both staying with the same friend. Michael is a social entrepreneur focused on driving innovations in sustainable practices. In particular, his energy goes toward those that relate to products and services which can enable a shift toward more sustainable lifestyles for everybody. His passion for impacting the health of the Ocean became absolutely clear to me over the next few days. He was in Thailand doing an environmental audit on the Starboard boards that carry the .Eco board logo. As I mentioned in an earlier chapter, Svein Rasmussen is passionate about mitigating his personal and corporate carbon footprint and is doing many proactive things to make that happen.

Michael and I happened to sit next to each other on the plane to Bali where we'd be surfing. He was reading a few magazines covering environmental topics. Our conversations during that plane ride ignited a fire in me that has focused my energy and ambitions toward being an ocean advocate.

Michael tells the story like this, "As I pulled out an environmental magazine to read on a plane ride to Bali, my seat mate Zane was full of questions. It wasn't a casual, 'What are you reading?' He was truly interested and curious. I have come to realize that is just the way Zane operates.

He asked questions about the magazines' environmental topics. Then on to the more important question, 'Why does that matter?' Zane has such a curious and open mind. It was apparent that he wanted to raise his voice and make a difference. I knew then that he would make a powerful ambassador for Sustainable Surf.

He listened intently as I explained the ocean issues for which Sustainable Surf works. The biggest is global warming and the way that warmer temperatures are causing water levels in the ocean to rise. I explained that we study the patterns and trends that are adding more energy to storms and even a change in seawater chemistry. Zane stayed focused and interested as I explained in more detail the causes making the oceans more acidic. The result of that acidic environment is negative to all life in the ocean."

The things Michael shared with me made such an impact. I felt the overwhelming sense of loss learning that 90% of the world's coral reefs could be extinct by 2030. One of four fish important to humans depends on coral reefs as their nursery. I told Michael how beautiful the reefs are near my home on Maui, at Launiupoko, Honolua Bay and Olowalu. Then Michael shared some statistics that hit home, literally.

Only 11% of my favorite home reefs remain from what they were 25 years ago. Think about it. That means that 89% of the reefs have disappeared in just the last 25 years. Suddenly I saw myself in the story. I had a heartbreaking but powerful "aha moment." I see how I connect to the situation and realize a definite role for me. I am all in. I need to make a difference. Sharing aloha is more than sharing stoke and goodwill. It is sharing a love for our environment on land, in the air and in the sea.

The next thing Michael explained to me was the impact of marine plastic. It's much more visual than the acidification of the ocean or the fact that the ocean is where we get two-thirds of our oxygen. The ocean, not trees, provide us with most of the air we breathe. While the plastic garbage we see on beaches is a problem, the worst problems are what we don't see.

Plastic is not biodegradable, but it does break down in sunlight. It is "photodegradable." It doesn't go away, but it does become a bigger danger when it is microplastic. It's like smog in the water and it impacts all sea life. From reefs, krill and plankton to dolphin, whales, sharks and birds – all marine life and the ocean food web is stressed by plastic.

By the time we made it to Bali, I had an entirely new understanding of a devastating problem. But it was time to go surfing. Michael and I were on the east side of Bali surfing at Changgu. It was a remote area with no facilities. Yet, as we surfed we were struck by all the trash in the water. We were both feeling upset by the "plastic tide." There had to be a better way. We kept talking after the surf session as we walked along the beach while, of course, picking up plastic as we went. We had no container to put the smaller pieces in – except in the pockets of our board shorts. At that moment, the "Pocket of Plastic Challenge" concept was born.

Journal Entry from August 2016 - Pocket of Plastic Challenge

8/21/16

This weekend I had a flight & great crowd for the
Clinic & SuperGrems clinic! Warren @ The Easy Cider
Set me up well after picking me up @ the airport. He got
Delnor to host me @ his place & it was comfortable &
refreshing to have some space to myself to get grounded &
relax! There were 9 ppl signed up including Delnor for
the pro Clinic, although I couldn't make it.
It was a small group but great because everyone learned
a lot; we went through boat control through paddle stroke,
buoy turns, tracking, & ability to maximize # of strokes on
each side & as well off course paddle stroke & technich for
efficiency... For the keiki ones we had about
4 kids & they were all so much fun & pure!
We started with a beach cleanup for the Pocket of Plastic
challeng to share w/ them the importance of being mindful of our
environment!.. Then we went onto the STP Starship all
together & had some fun teaching the importance of
"lokahi" (working together in harmony), basic paddle &
boast control & log rolling. One of the keiki' girls

Work is my norm. I have mad energy, insane energy,
a kind of stamina in terms of work that's a little crazy.

— Sidney Lumet, filmmaker

Michael spurred me on as the idea took form in my mind, "Zane had the idea that maybe we could make picking up plastic go as viral as the ALS Ice Bucket Challenge. Perhaps, 'pocket of plastic challenge' could be a way to make the problem more visible. It could be an on-ramp that would make it easier for more people to be aware of the problem and become involved. Just telling people about the problem of marine plastic is not enough to allow them to see themselves in the story. How amazing would it be if everyone realized they had an activist toolkit with them all the time? The simple act of picking up plastic and posting a photo online with hashtag #pocketofplastic could start a movement. We, at Sustainable Surf, strive to reach a key audience through the lens of surfing and ocean health. Marine plastic is the most visible problem."

From that day on I've shared the "Pocket of Plastic" idea with people young and old. As you're reading this I hope you join in. On the beach or in the water pick up the plastic, take a picture and share it on your social media with the hashtag #pocketofplastic. We can't do it all but we can all do something. That's our kuleana, our responsibility.

A Hawaiian word that goes hand in hand with "kuleana" is ha'aha'a. Its meaning is to be proud, by continuing well. So much of an athlete's life is wrapped up with training, events, mental and physical preparation and an environment of competition. Throughout this book you have gotten acquainted with my philosophies and attitude. In the end, my heart and soul are connected to the ocean. Competing for a prize, a win or a title means many things to many people. Winning doesn't imply being superior to someone else. In the Hawaiian culture, a true win develops from being superior to your previous self, modestly and humbly open to growth learned from others.

Ha'aha'a teaches us to groom our character with a humility stemming from the utmost of respect for others. Ha'aha'a helps us understand that no individual can satisfy every need. All in the 'ohana are needed. This was made incredibly clear to me when I spent time at the Parley for the Oceans - Ocean School. I felt like the lowest on the totem pole among so many scientists and well-known activists. By the end, I realized that I also have influence and networks. Through ha'aha'a, all are to be respected and supported for the talent and uniqueness they offer. The following stories have many aspects of ha'aha'a woven throughout them. Humility mixed with assertiveness, with a helping of bold adventure.

On February 18th 2016 as the world grieved the loss of surfing's most iconic big wave surfer, Brock Little, the swell of a lifetime came straight for the islands with more than ideal conditions. It was a day full of bold adventure, but also one that humbled us.

Matty recalls that day like this, "Zane and I woke up hours before sunrise and loaded our boat with Dad, Matt Bromley and Guy Mac. It was one of those days where you could feel the intense energy and mana from both the ocean and among ourselves. For the first time ever, we decided to launch our boat and jet ski on the northwest end of Maui and then travel around the north side. Our plan was to catch a few waves that have never been surfed before while on our way to Pe'ahi, aka Jaws.

The wind was calm and the sun was shining, yet the immense energy coming from the ocean could be felt deep in our gut. By the time we started rounding the North end of Maui, the waves had gotten bigger and bigger. We have always wanted to surf this wave break, but it was turning on fast and getting bigger with every set. We were the only ones around for miles and surfing one of the most dangerous and hard to reach waves we have always dreamed of. It was just Zane and me out in the water catching wave and wave.

Shortly before we decided to leave and start our journey to Jaws, we overheard an emergency call to lifeguards regarding an 18-year-old local who had been severely injured surfing alone at a wave just two miles away. We instantly knew it would be a friend of ours and backtracked to the location of the rescue. Luckily, the local lifeguards were able to get to him just minutes before we arrived. Just as we pulled up, they were leaving. It was an emergency situation to save the surfer's life. Unfortunately, it was as we had expected, when we saw it was our lifelong friend Nathan Schlea. He had braved the enormous swell alone. The accident had broken his femur in half and it was compounding out of his leg. It really was a lifesaving moment. But as the lifeguards took him away, we could not help but realize this wave was probably the best place on the entire island and there was absolutely no one else in the water. It wasn't as big as Jaws would have been, but it was picture perfect with probably 100 fewer people.

We wished our friend good luck, and quickly began one of the best sessions we have had to date. After just a few waves, we heard over the radio that DK Walsh (another one of our good friends and one of the modern-day big wave pioneers) had been injured at Jaws. He was being flown to the hospital on Oahu for a neck and back injury. We quickly realized the size and strength of the swell around the entire island chain and began to really take caution while surfing with this rising swell. After about thirty minutes of catching amazing waves and huge barrels, I watched from the channel as Zane dropped in on one of the biggest waves of the day and did not get his board set on rail correctly. He made a last-minute decision to straighten out and the entire ocean turned over and broke right on top of the back of his neck.

Luckily, he had a helmet and inflation vest on which probably saved his life. We watched as his board tomb-stoned for about 20 seconds then he finally rose to the surface in severe pain. My brother rarely likes to admit when he's hurt. He's the type of person that will break his arm and pretend like nothing happened until he thinks about it later on and realizes he needs to go to the hospital. But this was not the case. He was hurt, and hurt badly. All of our training and experience came into play as we secured his neck, loaded him on to the back of the jet ski, and drove him out past the surf to my father's boat.

There, we were able to assess the injury and make the decision to call off our plans to go to Jaws. We needed to get Zane to the hospital. It ended up being one of the hardest decisions we have ever made, as we knew it was the biggest, best and most hyped up swell of our entire lives. Matt Bromley, who had flown out from South Africa just for the swell, was absolutely itching to go to Jaws but helped make the decision to get Zane back to safety. He ended up in the hospital alongside several other surfers with severe neck and back whiplash that Zane renamed, "wavelash".

Luckily, that winter ended up being one of the best ever and we had many successful days out at Jaws, but none as big as the Brock swell. At the end of the day we were all very thankful to have made it out in one piece. We realized how many world class athletes were injured and hospitalized on that day. We were grateful that we didn't have any life-threatening injuries. We still think about that day, wondering if we would have caught the biggest waves of our lives at Jaws. But we had a day we will never forget, we tried something new, something different, and as always, we put it all on the line!"

Many times, Mother Nature and the ocean have delivered experiences to me that made me doubt my skills, face a fear and pause with hesitation. That description sounds like my inner feelings every time I cross the Pailolo Channel. The Pailolo Channel separates the islands of Maui and Moloka'i by just 8.5 miles at its shortest distance. With its almost perpetual rough waters and intense winds slamming waves against a canoe or standup board, it presents one of the most challenging channels in the Hawaiian Islands. Even the name, Pailolo, translates to "crazy channel."

Nothing can serve up humility like Mother Nature, especially on the ocean. While ha'aha'a urges us to be humble and to be modest, ha'aha'a does not promote holding back or a lack of assertiveness. Ha'aha'a recognizes there is merit in feeling proud of the good things you have done.

A day that dished out a hefty dose of humility and a quiet pride in our accomplishment was the day that my close friend Brennan Rose and I planned to paddle to Moloka'i and camp out. We didn't plan on paddling back to Maui. We were stoked on the camping trip. The plan was to visit Ekolu Kalama and then to surf, fish and hunt. We packed our open ocean SUP boards with fishing gear, camping gear and our short board surfboards strapped to the top of the nose. We weren't too worried about loading heavy because the Pailolo channel was blowing strong and we knew that we'd be going with the elements--downwind and down swell straight over to the east end of Moloka'i.

We launched from my Grandma Diane and Grandpa Hoyle's house in Kahana mid-morning. It was a beautiful day and the wind was blasting, just what we were hoping for. Brennan and I decided to drag lures on the way to Moloka'i and hopefully hook up on some dinner to bring to our host Ekolu Kalama. On the way over we had pretty good speed. Brennan and I were catching bump after bump edging through the wild and tough Pailolo channel.

I almost forgot we were still trolling lures because the downwind bumps were so fun. Then, all of a sudden, I realized Brennan wasn't near me. I stopped and turned around only to see him on his board, fighting a fish from his jimmy-rigged line and lure attached to a rubber slipper. It was the funniest image to look back and see him on his butt holding onto his rubber slipper for dear life as a mahimahi was jumping out of the water pulling him around. Finally, after a good fight for a bit, Brennan and the rubber slipper lost the battle to the mahimahi. The mahi swam off free of the lure. Nonetheless, an exciting element to our adventure was over.

Only about two and a half hours later we arrived to the east side of Moloka i at my uncle Scott Shoemaker's house. For a bit of back-story, my dad actually helped Scott build that house when he was my age. Dad would windsurf over every day to work on the house with Scott. At the end of the day they would windsurf back home. Now Brennan and I were following in my dad's path once again, aiming at that exact same point. We felt pretty good that we were reading the Pailolo channel well, allowing us to make it safely and swiftly.

That day we went hunting with Ekolu Kalama and our friend Chad Lima. Now, I am not a hunter by nature. I don't want to kill anything unless I eat it or share it with my family. In Hawai'i we grow up fishing, diving and hunting for our family's dinner. This was my first time deer hunting. Ekolu and Chad showed us around some ridges above Uncle Scott's house and not even 45 minutes into the drive Chad spotted some deer on the next ridge over. It was a long shot, but we pulled over and they set me up for my first ever attempt at deer hunting. Lying down on the ground, looking through the scope, I slowed my heart rate and steadied my breathing as I locked down the deer in the sight. I pulled the trigger and to my surprise saw the deer fall and roll part way down the steep ridge.

The boys were surprised with the shot, maybe it was just beginners luck. Now the hard part began; retrieving and tracking down dinner. Brennan and I hiked down the valley and across over to the next ridge line where we thought the deer was. It took us quite a bit of time to find it. When we did locate the deer, we came across the next challenge. How were we gonna hike this thing out?

I called Chad and Ekolu on my cell phone and they walked us through the process step by step. They explained where to cut the deer to gut it, enabling us to only carry out what we would be using. It was a very uncomfortable moment; Brennan holding my phone up with the volume on speaker phone, as Chad tried to lay it all out to me. He instructed, "Okay, now after you have made the cuts, stick your forearm in at least elbow deep and pull out the intestines and guts."

Brennan got the easy job, holding up the phone so I could hear the instructions. He had to laugh, looking at me. I was hesitant, hearing what I had to do. Part of my motivation to make this trip was for the experience of living off the land and providing for the people around me. This tough job was just part of the experience. We paid our respect to the deer and said a prayer thanking the deer for her life to feed my friends and me. I don't hunt or fish for sport. It is to feed my body and provide for others the nourishment we need to survive. I always pray and thank my catch for their sacrifice. I got the job done, but that wasn't even the hardest part.

Next, we started the long trek back, taking turns carrying the doe out. We ended up having to cut through some properties and kalo patches on our way out through the bottom of the valley. We ended up meeting with Chad and Ekolu back on the lower road, the only cement road around the island.

That afternoon I learned how to prepare the doe with Uncle Scott's neighbor, Robbert Seals. He is a Moloka'i local and has known me my entire life. He taught me how to clean and prepare the deer, then how to store and smoke it. Once it was all cleaned, we had to get the next course – some fresh-caught fish. Ekolu and I went out and set up a net in front of the house. Our fishing method with the net was to paddle around the net on our SUP boards and paipai to the water (slapping the water with our paddles). In less than 20 minutes we pulled the net in and had a few nice o'io (bonefish) to prep for dinner. We made fish cakes with the vegetables and eggs from the property and barbecued the deer while talking story through the night over some beers. It was an epic day.

The next morning, we woke up early with a wild plan to paddle AGAINST the wind and current across the Pailolo Channel back to Maui. Ekolu and Chad seemed to think it was kinda crazy and said no one had ever done it before. Maybe we were a bit cocky or maybe we just wanted to confront a challenge, but regardless, we didn't know what we were getting ourselves into.

Even though our idea to paddle the opposite way across the Pailolo Channel was radical, we did our best to set off with some planning. We drove up the coast upwind to Honouliwai, where we could get a better angle of the current and wind back to Maui. We started the paddle just after sunrise, as we were hoping to avoid the trade winds that usually come up mid-morning. A little over an hour into our paddle, Brennan looked at me with a face of pure uncertainty. I could sense the nerves, heck I felt it too. I turned around to see how far we had gone and to assess if it would be worth it to turn back.

We hadn't made too much ground, but that was expected. What was a disturbing surprise was looking over my shoulder only to see a thick lightning and thunder storm rolling down the east Moloka'i mountains toward the coastline and the channel. It was bearing down directly toward us. Now things started to get serious. Mother Nature seemed to be testing us. Or, maybe we had tested Mother Nature too much. I decided we should keep pushing forward, and then one more thing occurred to slow us down. I mean "one more thing" besides the

20-knot wind hammering us both on the side and straight in the face. One more thing beside the waist to chest-high rolling open ocean surf coming into us. This one more additional ingredient was my iPhone blasting off the hook.

The whole situation was "Victory at Sea." The wind and waves were pushing us backwards if you missed a stroke. So, stopping to sit down, take my backpack off and retrieve my phone was the last thing I was thinking about. Although the phone kept ringing, and I had a feeling it was my dad, I couldn't risk answering it. He probably had woken up to a text I sent him earlier that morning before starting the paddle back. He would be worried about the boat plan we texted to him as a safety measure. He knew the dangers of the Pailolo from so many crossings of the channel. He and my mom have had their share of "Victory at Sea" Pailolo experiences.

Finally, after dozens of calls, I stopped to answer the phone and was immediately losing ground. I was rapidly being pushed backwards as the waves slammed into me and the wind pushed my body, sitting on the board, like a sail. My dad had been waiting at Honolua point tracking us with binoculars for the last 45 minutes. He was desperate to tell me to watch out for the barge. The towboat was dragging a long chain that attached the barge to the tow. It was en route, dead set on our course. He told me that he would continue to watch and wait until we gave him a call to launch his boat to rescue us. He was a bit pissed and nervous, only because he knows the mana or power of the Pailolo channel very well. He has probably done more crossings on the channel than anyone else I know. It wasn't surprising that he was baffled that we decided to try to paddle back.

Even with all those obstacles Brennan and I were determined to finish the paddle. Despite the weather, current and wind pushing against us, then the additional challenge of the barge, we were determined to complete the crossing. Plus, I had all this frozen deer on my board that I needed to get home and into the freezer. By this time the meat was probably pretty thawed out and probably seemed like bait to any shark near us. I'm sure we had a few happy followers with the trail of blood we were releasing into the current.

We fought against the wind and waves with over 20 pounds of gear and deer meat on our boards for 6 hours and 40 minutes before we hit Maui's west side beach at a surf break called S-Turns. All the uncles on the beach were tripping on where we were coming in from on a day like that, with all kinds of camping, fishing and surf gear on top of our boards. It was classic. My dad, mom and grandparents were all relieved we had made it in safely. Their day had not been too easy. They spent all those hours waiting around playing "eye spy" with my grandparents in Kahana using their binoculars.

Brennan and I were beat by this time. Our vest pack for hydration had been long dry and our bodies were feeling the work and pain from the brutal paddle. My dad took Brennan and me back to my truck and soon we were on our way back to my house at Launiupoko. It was finally time to relax and smoke up the deer meat we had brought back to share with the 'ohana. There was one more chore and one I was happy to fulfill. I needed to clean the deer skin that I had brought back as a ho'omana'o mau, or memento, from my first deer hunt on Moloka'i. At the end of the day I looked back at the epic adventure where we faced some heavy challenges and obstacles that tested our endurance, resilience and ocean knowledge. I felt pride in accomplishing a fulfillment of the rewards that came from taking on a major challenge and putting myself, my comfort, and my confidence to the test.

Palena 'ole is the Hawaiian concept of our unlimited capacity and an invitation to live life without boundaries. Calm days with favorable wind, waves and currents always provide great emotional and spiritual experiences. Brennan and I created our abundance and another piece of our full life by reaching beyond what was comfortable and known. By preparing well and knowing both our capacity and limitations before embarking on the adventure, we honored our physical, intellectual, emotional, and spiritual capacity. We honored our resilience and relentless focus on our goal. Without a bit of arrogance, simply with a feeling of humility, we felt a great pride in what was accomplished through our adventure.

Surfing has taught me the importance of staying grounded and present in the midst of serenity and chaos alike.

Top photo from the Brock Little swell on the West Side Maui.

Bottom photo on one of the bigger lefts at Jaws
Top: Photo Credit: Matty Schweitzer / Mat5o Media. Bottom: Photo Credit: Mike Neal

CHAPTER NINE

Live in Your Present

A Personal Treasure

I was about 12 years old when I first started the practice of writing in a journal. Even at that age I was traveling across the world to competitions, having amazing experiences and meeting a widely diverse group of people. I was immersed in cultures new to me.

The normal routines and habits of a teen were not part of my life. I might be in three different countries to compete at two or three different events in a few weeks. My food, where I slept, and who I saw were all changing daily. In 2015 and 2016 alone I traveled to Canada, Costa Rica, Japan, Thailand, US Virgin Islands, British Virgin Islands, Bali, Australia, Dubai, New Zealand, Brazil, Abu Dhabi, Dominican Republic, Morocco, Finland, Netherlands/Holland, Spain, France, Italy, Germany, Austria, Ireland, Belgium, Fiji, Tahiti, Peru, Chile, Mexico and so many areas of the United States. Without some sort of ritual or routine it would have been easy to wear out or lose my focus.

For me I find so many rewards and value in journaling. Sometimes when on the road for the majority of the year, the biggest thing that gets to you is not having a routine, or consistency in your day to day life. This lack of routine puts you in a cloud or a daze when going through your days. Journaling keeps my head clear and my day consistent with a routine I can always rely on. Having over a decade of stories, journals, precious moments and relationships make me feel grateful for how far I have come. It's almost like a time capsule.

When I open a journal excerpt I am immediately taken back in time to that moment when I was writing in my journal. I relive the feelings

I felt when jotting my words and energy down. It really is a practice I appreciate. Similar to the practice of taking consistent steps toward a goal, journaling entry by entry, day by day, is fulfilling. Eventually you'll have made it to where you want to be.

Over more than a decade, so many of those experiences could have become a blur of memories. Because of my day to day habit of writing in my journal I'm able to go back and remember the focus and conviction to my goals I have had across the years. My mind could not have such clear memories of both the important events as well as the very ordinary days on its own. I don't write a lot daily, but through cues in my journal I have bits of my days, my life, written down. Having all those journals is like a treasure. Sometimes I might have written for just a few minutes a day. Other times I wrote a dozen pages.

Throughout this book you've experienced so many stories that have made me who I am. You've gotten to know me. This chapter is my invitation to you, to get to know you better through your stories. How much you write is not as important as the regular practice. That's how a habit is built. Keeping a consistent journal has let me notice where my energy and attention has been focused. That focus has made such a powerful impact on where my journey has carried me.

It's next to impossible to share or explain the power of a consistent practice of being mindful and writing down your thoughts. Journaling is not about trying to change or improve your life. Simply being awake, aware and reflecting with gratitude delivers what you need and prepares you to receive it. Investing time regularly in writing with mindfulness, seeking inspiration and innovation in big and small things allows you to be the teacher – and the student – for your own life lessons. Small steps build a life. Your own reflection, energy and power will allow you to create a life of purpose and passion.

Tapping into that energy takes some discipline and a consistent practice.

There is joy, good fortune and luck everywhere, but it can be missed when day-to-day demands, a busy life, challenges, or frustration demand your attention. We have the power over choices, and in our own way we develop strategies that are ours alone, strategies that can make each day better. Some nights I fall into bed exhausted to the core. I lie there with a nagging need to write in my journal. I know the value my consistent habit has had on my life and I also know how easy it would be to let that habit lapse. Inevitably, I will drag myself out of bed, open my *Five Minute Journal* (published by Intelligent Change) to write and reflect on my day. Even on the days when I have to force myself to write, I choose to examine what was awesome, what I could have done to make the day even more amazing and steps I made toward a goal.

Even when I skip a day, I will go back and think about that day and make notes for it, I have been doing this for so long that even when I am not journaling, I am thinking about what I would be writing. Choices and days gathered together create a life. By journaling you will not miss the part you play in relentlessly pursuing your dreams every day.

Sometimes we are so busy doing, striving, and achieving that some of the big things get lost. We cannot afford to lose even some of the simple, little things that matter so much. It's funny but our lives may be determined less by actual past events than by the way we remember them. In this chapter, I will talk a lot about the practice of mindful gratitude. But something that is almost as powerful is the collection of ordinary life stories that your journal will provide.

Here's an example of one of my journal entries from November of 2008. In the scope of all the wild and crazy adventures I've had with my dad and his friends, this one memory might have lost something over time. But when I re-read it now, almost a decade later, I can still feel the excitement and fun I enjoyed.

The next part is directly from my Journal of 11/19/08- 11/21/08: My Dad was hired by Paul Ehman Productions to help with the CBS show, "The Amazing Race." I was about 13 and I got to go along just for the fun. Our job was to set about 100 buoys for the contestants.

Their first challenge was landing in Kahului and rushing with their rental car to the harbor where they then found a jet ski. They had to drive the jet ski, flying around the island to the Pali coast where they would find the hundreds of buoys we'd anchored to the bottom along the Pali cliff line. Each of them had a clip but just one of them was the mystery clip that had the clue. They had to go to all the buoys in order to find the right one. Some of the contestants were lucky and got the right one immediately. Others were not so clever when searching underwater and it took them a really long time to get to all the buoys.

We laid 100 buoys against the NaPali cliff. Greg Aguera was with us and it was really fun. We tied over 200 bowline knots for the anchors and buoys. After we finished work for the day, my Dad and I slept there anchored for one night. That evening we night-dove and we were scared of sharks because it was a new area where we had never done a night-dive before.

I caught my first lobster, menpachi and rock bass. The lobbie (lobster) I grabbed and the fish I speared square in the head. My Dad caught another lobster and a huge 711 crab. I saw an octopus in a hole but could not get it.

We went back to the boat with our catch. My dad had brought this George Forman grill and we were there out on the water, under the stars, grilling our fresh catch and living like kings. Before we went night diving we saw dinoflagellates. A dinoflagellate is a type of plankton that glows at night because it has bioluminescence. My Dad had seen lots of these before, but this was my first time. They were lighting up the water with sparkling silver and blue shining everywhere. I remember feeling such a sense of being one with nature, but also being awestruck by its beauty.

We slept on the boat out under the stars. We had casted the nets a lot all day and would be doing that the next day too. I was tired and happy.

Directly from my Journal on 11/20/08: We were able to fish a lot today. We adjusted a few buoys and that was about it for work. Fishing was great. We used this rig that required "whipping" the line out with a powerful cast and retrieving it back in. We did some diving until the weather started to change. A big storm was coming so we moved our anchor further out. It was getting rough, nothing like the night before. So that night we went to Maalaea to sleep in the boat slip of my dad's friend, Doug Hunt, because it was too rough where we had been.

11/21/08: We worked all day on the jet skis for the filming of the show, *The Amazing Race*. When it was over, Bryce's dad, Grant Henry, and I went out on his ski and picked up all 5 rows of 20 buoys. There were 2 anchors on each row. Then we put them in Dad's boat so Dad and Greg could untie all the bowlines, anchors, clips and buoys. Grant and I drove back to Māʻalaea on the jet ski pushing 60 mph.

New Perspective and Reflection: Reading back over your journal you will have the opportunity to remember what your days, your life, has offered. I am sometimes surprised to read back over things that I've acknowledged with appreciation and gratitude. Our lives may be determined less by the actual past events than by the way we remember them.

I know for sure that appreciating whatever shows up for you in life changes your personal energy. The mindful practice of acting from a space of gratitude around my life experience has changed me. I am absolutely sure that it also changed many outcomes, goals – and who I am. Paying attention to my progress, instead of solely focusing on the big goals or the big wins, actually has become a process of being aware of who I really am and what gives me the most satisfaction, happiness, and sense of my true purpose.

The Universe tries to tell us the truth. From a 2015 journal entry I can look back on a decision that might have been a subconscious influence on future events. I wrote about the day that I stopped wearing my silver chain. This was inspired by a friend who told me, "You should get rid of that silver chain because you deserve Gold, Champ." It was such a simple statement, but it had a profound impact on me.

This particular day was at the time I had finished 2nd overall on the Standup World Tour in 2015. I finished just shy of the World Champion title I'd been chasing for years. I was always in the top four over all, but hadn't won the overall title yet. It was before I became the World Champion by winning the ISA Worlds in Sup surfing in 2016. There was a subconscious thought process that took place from then on, and even before I took the silver off. I had been used to wearing the silver chain 24/7. Once I took it off I didn't wear anything around my neck for a while. When I went on to win the Ultimate Waterman (story in Chapter One) in New Zealand, I was presented with my Pounamu necklace. I believed it was meant to replace my silver chain symbolically for a GOLD. It represents victory and also reminds me of the mana within me and around me. The "Hei Matau," or hook, design in Polynesian culture represents safety over water, abundance and the ability to provide..

Like anything worth learning or worth doing, creating your journal story takes practice and commitment. Feel what you write and remember that what you write is for you, by you and there is no right or wrong content. I write from my heart and I know, in my heart, that each day I am doing the best I can.

Am I perfect? Absolutely not! Dave Kalama is a legendary waterman and a person I respect very much. He has shared lessons with me throughout my life. Sometimes I listened and learned, but sometimes I had to do it the hard way and figure things out on my own. A good friend will share things that aren't easy to hear, but are useful for insights and perspective as we strive to be our best selves.

Dave describes me like this, "When I think of Zane as a younger kid what comes to mind is his abundance of unharnessed energy. That energy mostly serves him well, but as he was maturing it was almost like a borderline problem, flirting with being a negative. With his headstrong way of figuring things out for himself, not all experiences have gone well. But he is becoming much more focused and wiser, even at his relatively young age. Being innovative and pioneering isn't a one-off situation. Zane is fortunate to have a mindset open to experimenting, tweaking and being willing to fail. Zane's innovation, spirit, and bold risk-taking will, hopefully, be balanced by being smart. The combination is all part of his life journey

Zane has a natural inclination to share his knowledge. He comes from a great family that has been instrumental in inspiring him to be the really good person he is. That is one of the key defining characteristics he has to his core. For his age and his energy level, he has come a long way toward being a true master, but he's not there yet.

Right now, Zane, along with others like Kai Lenny, are defining the 'new school' waterman. He possesses a lot of traditional waterman skills. The face and definition of the classic way of being a waterman is changing and Zane is the epitome of that evolution."

Dave knows me well and his insight is valued. While Dave mentioned my "unharnessed energy," my grandmother, Carolyn, called it "enthusiasm overload." As I mentioned in an earlier chapter, I earned the nicknames, "Zaniac" and "InZane" at a very young age. Every life offers us many ways to "Learn from your past." I know that I definitely have!

I have made choices that could have endangered myself and others. I take responsibility for bad decisions, like those that led to my fall from the cliff in Peru, but the things that hurt me most is when a poor choice or decision harms others. If you gathered my family and friends around they could tell plenty of stories about me that would make me cringe. I will share one story that still hurts me even to this day. I would love to be able to do that day over, to make a different choice.

I was visiting my brother, Matty, in Santa Barbara. I was staying at his friend's house. I offered to take their little chihuahua out for a walk. I really liked that little dog, he had been like my little buddy that trip. They were so happy for me to take it for a walk since they were so busy and didn't usually have time to walk him. They gave me the collar and leash. I put them on the dog and we headed to the beach.

We took a little run at the beach, and he had a great time playing. On the way back from the beach, we were about to cross the street when the dog had a bit of a freak out. He backed up. As he was pulling backwards the collar slipped over his head and off. The dog ran out into the street and got run over by a car. I remember the scream of the dog. I ran over and picked the dog up, cradling him in my arms as he bit my hands and arms over and over again. The poor thing had just gotten flattened. It was crying and biting me. It broke my heart to see that.

I ran him back to the house and we took him to the vet as fast as we could. The nurse said sometimes dogs can take a quick impact like that and survive. There were no fractures to the bones. We hoped for the best and brought the little dog home. I had to leave the next day. Two days later I learned that it had died. I felt so bad. It was my kuleana to take care of that dog. It was more than a dog to our friends, it was a part of their family and they were devastated. I thought of all the ways I could have prevented it from happening. I could have checked the collar, I could have held the dog as we crossed the street. Unfortunately, I didn't. Now I have to carry that mistake and pain with me.

At the end of each day I have the chance to reflect on a list of amazing things and the not so amazing things that have happened. The final reflection is my chance to recognize that I have control over my day, my progress and my growth. The final thing I write is how I could have made my day even better. The prompts help me write with details and honesty. The details create a better story, one that will become your treasure when you look back over your journal weeks or years after your entry.

Here's an example of a very great day that I could have made even better. The day was September 28, 2016 the day the SUP awards were announced. SUP magazine created the SUP Awards as standup paddling's top honor, recognizing the absolute best that the sport has to offer. The editorial staff collects nominations from readers and fans over the first half of the year. The same people then vote for their favorites online.

The day before the event I was in Dana Point with members of the Starboard team, and distributors from all over the world. My gratitude list included, "being a valued member of the Starboard team, happy that the distributor meeting was in San Diego, and for all the great connections and impressions being made there."

When I thought about what would make the day great, one thing I listed was "being all organized and confident with my financial and work business." I balanced that with "Having fun with Connor Baxter and doing some training." Another thing I put into words and write down each morning is an affirmation. Most affirmations begin with "I am," but I also write from the point of "I know," "I love," or "I have." An affirmation doesn't come a place of want or need, so I wouldn't begin with, "I want."

On September 27, I began my day by writing, "I am in a great position of life with so much opportunity and love." And off I went on my day. By the time the day was over and I wrote about amazing things that happened that day I listed, "Getting to host a hydrofoil clinic, feeling appreciation from everyone, and helping to present for Rayvolt bikes." How the day was amazing balanced nicely with my morning hopes for the day.

How could I have made the day even better? I wrote, "By doing foundation training and stretching." There is always something that could have made the day better and it is written without judgment, but with an awareness of growth and even more potential.

The next day it was a no-brainer to write what would make the day great, "Winning an award at the SUP Awards and having a good last day with the Starboard team. My affirmation was, "I am humble." After an incredible awards night, I was so happy reflecting on the amazing day. I wrote, "I won an award for Male Paddler of the Year (2nd place), I got 4 Rayvolt bikes to bring home and my friend Brennan had a nice dress shirt for me to wear at the SUP awards."

How could I have made the day better? Nothing earth-shattering, "By doing some yoga and taking a nap."

You will discover surprises and opportunities exposed when you go over your journal. When life seems boring or mundane, journaling can remind you of excitement, emotions, and moments of inspiration.

The more you do this, the more you'll start to really appreciate what a gift your life is. Daily reflection and the pure activity of writing from your spirit changes you in ways you cannot even imagine at the start

In addition to journaling about what I am grateful, I also write my goal for the day. The goal might be something that will takes months or years to attain, or it could be something I can complete in a day. I have big goals and ideas, but documenting small steps and progress helps build momentum and gratitude. Very little of what any of us want to do can be done alone or without daily action.

I have three journals. One is a training journal with notes about work-outs, equipment and new techniques I learn. Another is a blank page journal in which I write longer stories, usually reflections of an event or experience written afterward. That's often on a long flight home when everything is fresh in my mind. The journal I use every day has simple prompts for morning and evening reflection. Specifically, I use one called the *Five Minute Journal*, created by Alex Ikonn and UJ Ramdas (Publisher, Intelligent Change).

The first thirty pages of that journal are filled with insights that can increase your understanding of how journal writing daily can positively impact your life. Some of the points most meaningful to me are summarized from their journal (with permission) below.

By keeping a daily journal, you'll have a snapshot of your days, weeks, months and years. It's like looking at pictures from years ago. They bring nostalgia, a smile and a flood of memories. Imagine if you could have that same experience by just flipping to a certain day in a specific year in your life.

The *Five Minute Journal* isn't magic, you still have to do the work, get out of your comfort zone, take action and make the magic happen. The *Five Minute Journal* is your guide. Are you ready? It has often been said that if you let the Universe know what you want, it will come your way. The same is true of your subconscious. Thomas Edison said it this way, "Never go to sleep without a request to your subconscious."

In addition, the *Five Minute Journal* invites daily practice of gratitude. It defines that simply as, "Gratitude is the experience of counting one's blessings." A 2003 study by Emmons and McCullough found that keeping a daily gratitude journal leads to better sleep, reductions of physical pain, a greater sense of well-being and a better ability to handle change.

A second daily cue is, "What would make today great?" Over time, by writing about the things over which you have control, you actually open the door to specific actions you can accomplish. While you might love a sunny day or glassy surf at your favorite break, you can't control that. Really thinking about what would make a great day has been one of my favorite parts of my journal practice. Over time I have gotten better at deciding what to write. As the years have passed, it's obvious that I have been changing and moving forward. I look back and realize all I have learned from my past. Just as important is living in my present, 100% aware and mindful. Journaling is a powerful tool for making that happen.

At the end of your day, be proud of the steps you've taken towards your goals and desired future. Windsurfing at my home break on the West side of Maui at DT Flemings Beach.
Photo Credit: Dooma Photos

CHAPTER TEN

Manifest your Future

Throughout the book I've shared quotes and maxims that have resonated with me and have helped me stay on track with my attitude and motivation. Being present and mindful is a huge part of how I live life to its fullest. Another key aspect of the heart and spirit that is "me" is the honor of being Hawaiian-born. I study the language and maintain a close relationship with people and groups working to keep the Hawaiian language, traditions and culture thriving across generations.

A life is created by our past, our present and our future. I often repeat a phrase that brings balance and meaning to me. It is, "Learn from your past, live in your present and manifest your future."

For me, my past is made up of a powerful blend of my personal past, the past of my family and the past that created the Hawaiian culture. Hawaiian culture is a rich and powerful force in my life. Respecting our oceans, our land, each other and ourselves makes sense.

Hawaiians say that we can live a life in this way by making "pono" choices. Pono choices are described as righteous and balanced. Throughout this book I've shared my stories. In some, I made pono choices, in others – well, I shared stories from age 11 to the present day. Of course, there were some bumps in the road. However, in all of the stories there is a consistent and powerful thread - the ocean.

I can't imagine my life without the ocean. Throughout my career I have been able to share what I love through InZane SUPer Grom clinics around the globe. The kids sometimes need to learn to swim before they surf. While they are exposed to surfing and paddling, they also learn how much the ocean needs our love and care. I make sure we don't have single use plastic at the clinics by providing aluminum water bottles for each child donated by my clothing sponsor, Honolua Surf Company. My hope is to inspire the kids and their families to continue to use those water bottles and make a choice not to use plastic water bottles again. Part of the day always includes a beach cleanup so we always leave the beach cleaner than we found it.

When I share my "Aloha" program at schools (more in Chapter 7) the message and my intent is to inspire the students with stories that remind them of how important a connection to nature is to their lives. Hopefully, they will realize the power of their influence and share the message with their friends and family. Any teacher will tell you that the most innovative problem-solvers in any group of young people are those that can imagine solutions and ways of thinking that are often inspired in surprising ways.

I make a choice every day to seek ways that I can innovate and inspire – myself and others. Sometimes things align in a way that connects where we want to go with opportunity. As I mentioned earlier in the book, I had the almost unimaginable honor of being one of the influential individuals invited to the Maldives for a trip with Parley for the Oceans to attend the Parley Ocean School early in 2017. Cyrill Gutsch is a German-born and world-renowned designer and creative entrepreneur based in New York City.

In 2012, a meeting with activist, Captain Paul Watson of the Sea Shepherd Conservation Society and co-founder of Greenpeace, convinced Cyrill to take on the most challenging client; the world's oceans. He did that with the particular objective of focusing attention on the multiple threats facing this vital ecosystem and on establishing a new business culture where it is more lucrative to protect the oceans than to destroy them.

This is from the Parley for the Oceans website, Jacques Cousteau said, "People protect what they love." But before you can love something you need to know it, and there's no better way to learn than through total immersion within the blue universe we're fighting to preserve and protect. This belief guides the curriculum of Parley Ocean School, a unique program blending ocean activism with learning and exploration on, around, and in the marine environment.

I spend most of my life in, on or under the ocean. However, I had no idea how much I didn't know about the ocean and the scope of the devastation plastic is causing. Through a series of global marine expeditions, Parley Ocean School (POS) is educating and empowering ambassadors for what might seem like an impossible mission. Each session of POS is dedicated to deepening scientific understanding of marine cultures and environments, with a focus on promoting stewardship, awareness, and solutions in local communities. Every POS alumni leaves with a renewed understanding of their role in this world, and of the actions they can take to protect it in the office, by the sea and at home. I was completely inspired to become the best ocean-advocate I could be after the experience at this Parley Ocean School.

As a waterman following generations of my own family in their connection to, not only the ocean, but also the air, the wind and nature, it is completely natural for me to have a vision of a healthy vibrant ocean. For many who visit the ocean infrequently, or maybe only while on vacation, it looks like a healthy, vibrant ecosystem. But, compared to what?

The term "shifting baseline syndrome" is an expression coined by fisheries scientist, Daniel Pauly. It describes the memory loss from one generation to the next. As one generation disappears, so does the knowledge of what once was. If a child never hears about the way a forest, a snow covered peak or the ocean was a generation or two ago, that memory is lost. Since birth I have been blessed with hearing stories and memories from my 'ohana. Our family stories recall the way the ocean was twenty, forty or more years ago. Think about young people who are the second or third generation of families not connected to either the ocean or to nature.

By being disconnected from the past, we are also disconnected from the future. As aware as I am, being in the ocean every day I can be, I was not 100% aware of the dire situation that is the health of the oceans. While at Parley Ocean School, I was shocked by the story of plastic and the devastating impact it has on the environment. One species that demonstrates this sad situation is the albatross. I watched the film *Albatross* produced by Chris Jordan and it affected me in both my heart and my gut.

While a huge part of the plastic debris is washing up on beaches where it can be collected relatively easily like we do at beach clean-ups, the majority of the plastic has broken down into small pieces 1/4 of an inch or smaller. The plastic trash is scattered over massive areas and is not easily visible or collected. But seabirds find it.

Albatross is a powerful visual journey into the heart of an environmental tragedy. On one of most remote islands on Earth, Midway atoll or Pihemanu, tens of thousands of albatross chicks lie dead on the ground, their bodies filled with plastic. Returning to the island over several years, Chris and his filming team witnessed cycles of birth, life, and death of these magnificent creature. It was a story that clearly illustrated how disconnected most of us are to what is happening due to our love affair with plastic. I deeply felt the experience of beauty and love for the miracle of life on Earth by watching his film.

Chris Jordan says the albatross has been around for millions of years and for the majority of that time they didn't have to distinguish what they could and could not ingest.

"Today, instead of coming home with a stomach full of squid these birds are coming home with a stomach full of lighters and other plastic objects," he says. (Trailer for his film is here http://www.chrisjordan.com/gallery/midway-film/#trailer)

Because they travel so far, the albatross is an "incredible indicator species." Chris explains it like this, "When you see large decline in the albatross population that is a huge wakeup call that something is happening to our planet."

But there is more to the story than just dying birds, according to Jordan, which is why he decided to make the film. In addition to documenting the death of the birds he explains that he wanted to capture what he sees as the essential beauty of the bird when it's alive.

Chris Jordan's project touched my heart so much that I actually began to work on a children's picture book based on the albatross. But my strongest asset is not as a writer of children's books. In fact, I never saw myself as a novelist before being challenged to write this book by my grandmother Carolyn, and with the invaluable assistance from our family friend and ocean enthusiast, Judy Shasek, of Water Words. After experiencing Parley Ocean School, thinking about the best way I could use my influence and my network was my challenge. It required innovation to discover how I can best use my experience and talents to impact people in my own way.

The oceans are dying. But it's not too late to save them. Only passion and creativity on a collaborative level will end marine plastic pollution. Cyrill Gutsch shares The Parley A.I.R. Strategy as a way to addresses the fast-growing and global threat of plastic pollution based on the belief that plastic is a design failure, one that can only be solved if we reinvent the material itself. He shares, "We all have a role to play in the solution. Let's invent our way out of this mess. Together."

I know that Cyrill is right. We need to do this "together." Even before returning home from Parley Ocean School my action had begun. One by one I spoke with my sponsors and explained the need to re-invent and re-design from packaging to product. It was fantastic to hear ideas from my sponsors immediately. Some had already taken steps towards eco innovations such as Starboard teaming up with Sustainable Surf, Parley for The Ocean and Water Trek to combine innovative quality with an alternative means of production using environmentally friendly materials. Beyond that, Starboard is making a huge commitment to take away damage that has already been done by planting one mangrove tree for every single Starboard product sold. A mangrove's lifespan has the potential to remove 1 ton of CO_2 from our atmosphere. The tree's roots act as a filtration system in the water and ground. In addition, it's an ecosystem and refuge for small fish. The roots stretch into the ground almost like a protective cage. (See more on www.star-board-blue.com)

What challenges align with your life mission and the path toward manifesting your future? Who are the creators and collaborators you can influence and inspire? What tools are available to reinvent and redesign the journey, the solutions, and your dreams?

The connections you need, the opportunities, and the tools are available. Learning from your past and living authentically in your present requires mindful observation and reflection on every day, no matter how ordinary or challenging it might seem at the time. I've learned that my dedication to capturing my moments, experiences, and emotions in my journal has led to major success in following my dreams and keeping on track with achieving them. Journaling has kept me grounded and present in the midst of my life's chaotic routine.

I began work on this book project as a means to "begin a conversation with many people. The process proved to me how important it is to not only consistently work towards our dreams by keeping them locked in our heart and in our minds, but also by taking action toward achieving them. My friend and mentor, Suzie Cooney always says, "The mind wins first." That's accomplished by taking a step towards your goals every day – even if it's just the smallest step. As important is believing in yourself. This book has reassured me that life, our struggles, and endeavors are stepping stones, and that every step truly does matter. Everything is unfolding just as it should – just as my grandma Carolyn would always tell me!

The stories of my life, of your life, are created by how we choose to live. For me to feel truly balanced I need to live life standing strong for what is pono – not only for myself, but also for the greater good, for my environment, and for my loved ones. My life is at its best when I live with respect for the land and for the sea – my home. Preparing for the future is key to who I might become. It's interesting that making the video project, "Zane's Deep Blue Life," with my brother, Matty, Michael Stewart, and Hoku Haiku, began with the chance for me to "Learn from my past" and share a powerful message.

I had the high honor of working with Hoku Haiku, a cultural educator who teaches programs to groups ranging from Boy Scouts working toward their Hawaiian badge to law school students. The programs he runs focus on raising cultural awareness by getting people to connect back to the land and nature. My past includes generations of people connected closely and strongly to the ocean and the land of Hawai'i. We are living on a wonderful planet, at an amazing time where each of us can make a difference through pono decisions. Many decisions we make daily may not seem "major," but minor decisions such as using single use plastics add up to major issues. So, it's important to be present and catch ourselves asking whether the decisions we are making daily are pono.

The "Deep Blue Life" project was brought about by Michael Stewart, founder of Sustainable Surf. He created the campaign and lifestyle initiative, "Deep Blue Life" with Starboard and wanted this to be a widely shared video to inspire people how to take a step towards a deep blue life themselves. The story is told through the language, knowledge and cultural wisdom of ancient Hawai'i. I had the honor to live a "dawn to dusk" day in the film, roaming my modern home ground and ocean playground, in harmony with the sustainable lifestyle system. That system was developed thousands of years ago by Hawaiians.

The ancient wisdom of Hawai'i's Ahupa'a system has plenty to teach us all about how to live a more engaged, meaningful and stoked-up life, one that enriches and preserves your community and environment while giving you plenty of time to play. The lessons are relevant whether you play in the waves or through your creative work, life, and dreams. (Link for video: star-board-sup.com/2017/zanes-deep-blue-day-sustainable-surf)

I strive daily to be a pioneer, not daunted by what might seem to be an impossibility. I learned from my father, Matt, who turned Windsurf Freestyle into an extreme sport. I have also watched family friends like Brett Lickle and Dave Kalama take ideas and turn them into reality with all my favorite water sports.

I have so much gratitude for all the waterman pioneers whose innovations have inspired generations that include my generation and the next ones coming up behind us. Being recognized by someone like Brett Lickle is humbling and an honor. Brett was kind to share these words, "If you enter a room and Zane Schweitzer is there, you will know it immediately. His smile radiates from one side of the room to the other. Zane is one of the gifted few who was born to do exactly what he's doing. He comes from a family of world class athletes. Not only did Zane have to compete with his older brother, Matty, but he also had to compete with both his mother and father. Zane has matured into quite a gentleman and ambassador for our planet. He is one of an elite few, like Kai Lenny, Albee Layer, Dusty Payne, Matt Meola and Kai Barger that are all from Maui and pushing surfing to the next level." Brett, Dave, and of course, Laird Hamilton, were the ones always pushing the limits to change things up. They pioneered the sports of tow-in surfing, kitesurfing and big wave surfing with a passion for innovation They truly revolutionized the water sports I love so much. They are relentless in following their dreams and manifesting their ideas. Rush Randle and Alex Aguera did the same for hydrofoiling. Now it's our turn. I have had so much fun pioneering standup paddling and hydrofoiling. The next chapter will undoubtedly include the role of being an ocean advocate.

The people I have the honor to spend time with and the experiences that come from saying, "Yes" to challenges have helped to develop that pioneering spirit in me. I have the opportunity to "live in my present" by actively "learning from my past." One example is the recent Maui 2 Molokai (M2M) Challenge in July of 2017.

In July of 2017 I hydrofoiled to Moloka'i from Maui for a race called Maui 2 Molokai organized and founded by Claire Mawae to raise money for the Youth of Moloka'i. By completing this race, I became the first person to ever complete the Pailolo Crossing in a race on a hydrofoil. At the awards ceremony, Claire reminded me that I had also pioneered the first Sup crossing in the same race a decade earlier.

It was nice to talk with her and hear her praise about being courageous back when I was about 14, in 2008, when I decided to standup paddle across the Pailolo Channel during the windsurf race. At that time in 2008, the Maui 2 Molokai race was mostly a windsurfing and kitesurfing race – all wind sports. Standup paddling was just starting to pick up momentum in my life. Maui councilwoman, Ellie Cochran, had contacted my mom and asked if the three of us would like to team up to standup paddle across and raise money for the kids in the process. That was the first year. Ellie, Connor Baxter and I pioneered standup paddling in that race. My dad had the boat out for escorting, so we all felt safe.

We became the first to paddle the channel and the first ever in a race. We presented a check to Maui's "Youth in Motion" for $5,000. Claire said that us entering that race and Connor and I as young keiki being able to conquer it, created momentum for the following years. The event has now evolved into being a world renowned standup paddling race. Unfortunately, they don't do the windsurfing crossing any more.

It was a similar feeling this year, in 2017, sitting with my unlimited board on the beach at D.T. Flemings. I was listening to the riders' briefing, looking at the conditions, while trying to stay focused on the horizon. I was studying the conditions to determine if the surf conditions would provide big enough bumps to surf across on my 6'9" hydrofoil that was still in my truck. My friends and top standup paddlers, James Casey, Kody Kerbox, Josh Riccio, and the other Elite athletes continued to egg me on to, "Send it on the foil!"

I had left my foil in the truck because when I first got to Flemings Beach it didn't seem to be very windy. Just before the start after the riders' briefing we did a pule, a prayer. Andy Claydon did the blessing and asked me to do a few words in Hawaiian. After we finished, I walked to the water's edge and called in one of the lifeguards who was on the jet ski close to shore. I asked him to take me out to the wind line.

Once we got out to the wind line I told him, "Okay, that's enough. I've seen what I need to see"

I went straight in, threw my hydrofoil together really quick in like six or seven minutes and just made it in time to the start line before the start of the race. It was a paddle in the beginning, for sure. I was all excited at the beginning of the race and I was able to pop up the foil on a flat-water fly in Flemings Bay. Pumping like that didn't last long. I thought about the distance ahead. I had 26 miles to go and I needed to conserve my energy.

I ended up paddling the little 6'9" board out to the wind line while all the other guys on the race boards were passing way out in front of me. Once I finally got to the wind line, about 25 minutes after the start, I was able to start to catching bumps. I remember just having so much fun just surfing these waves all the way across. I realized that I needed to start edging more toward Moloka'i. I had been getting lost with the rides and before I knew it I was heading very much toward Lanai which was the direction the bumps were going. I was trying to follow the bumps because I didn't want to work my back leg pumping the board too much.

Eventually I did have to start edging more toward Moloka'i and that only added to my fatigue. I started cramping big time in my back leg after a good hour of surfing, of just flying. All of a sudden, I just had to really start getting upwind. Luckily the escort boat was right there and was able to take me upwind toward Moloka'i. This took me backwards on the course but at least I was placed further from Lāna'i and closer to Moloka'i. Those last ten miles or so after Kamalo were so much fun. It was complete surfing, just full speed carving on these big rolling swells.

Foiling really is a serene feeling. To be up there all the friction of the board is released off the surface. The splashing of the water becomes almost silent and all you hear is the wind in your ears and a slight buzz of the foil under the water. Being able to just surf and connect the dots for so many miles until I got to Kaunakakai was incredible. I went a little too far in near to the finish at Kaunakakai, thinking I could catch a wave off the end of the reef before the pier. The tide was a bit low so I had to paddle back out through the lagoon and ended with about 30 minutes paddling the 6'9" into the finish. But, everything in-between was surfing.

I thought back to 2008 when I was one of the first people in the M2M competition to standup paddle across the channel. I believe that in the very near future we're going to see a movement creating strong momentum for foiling across the same Maui 2 Molokai race. I foresee a future that will include foiling and many other open ocean styles of racing. We might even see more people foiling than standup paddling, especially in open ocean downwind races such as the M2M, because it allows one of the best runs of rolling swells in the world.

How does change like this happen? In any walk of life, those who innovate and inspire learn from their past. In fact, they learn from the past of all the pioneers in their niche who follow their same passion. Relentlessly following my dreams has taken me to over 50 countries around the globe. I have had the opportunity to see some of the most beautiful places imaginable while meeting incredible people from so many different cultures and walks of life. Most recently, because of the huge curiosity around foiling, I traveled around the East Coast of the US hosting InZane Clinics for Sup surf and foil lessons. Each day I met people on and off the water and was both impressed and surprised by their passion for water sports and their sense of community.

While I was seen as a pioneer in foiling, an innovator in the surf and somewhat of an expert in Sup technique, I may have learned as much, or more, than the clinic participants.

Concluding words

The clinics I hosted during the summer and fall of 2017 allowed me to share my vision of making a difference in the world. My journal entries from those days were powerful reminders of how a relentless pursuit of dreams can "manifest your future." After spending almost my entire life training and competing for a place on the podium, my heart is guiding me toward adding a different sort of "podium" to my vision and goals. For more than a decade I have been chasing the "Gold" – victories. During that time, I have had the opportunity to speak with various groups and share motivation through my stories. I have come to realize that I can use my talents and expertise in a quest toward two very different types of podiums.

The ocean and the sports I practice in that environment are much more than activities or sports. While on the water I connect with nature, practice mindfulness and enjoy the relentless pursuit of what I'm most passionate about. That's what motivates me to keep on believing and creating. The ocean and water sports that have created the bond connecting me to this powerful environment have also taught me so many hidden values. My pursuit has enlightened me with so many reasons to continue learning from our environment, as well as sharing the joy the ocean can bring to your life. With the joy and the benefits we reap from our environment, hopefully the importance of a responsibility emerges. I commit to using my voice, my connections and my time to take care of our "playground," our environment! I invite you to join me. Mahalo e ke Akua, mahalo e moana!

Where will the future lead me? I can only continue to "Believe and Create," to "Innovate and Inspire." I know for certain that sharing whatever influence I have and allowing my voice to be heard is in my future. Making a difference in my family, within my community and for the environment is something each of us can accomplish in our own way. All this is part of chasing my goals.

This book began with an introduction to me and an invitation to explore "beneath the surface" of my life's journey on and off the water. You've gotten some insight to the motivations, dreams, goals, choices and influences in my life that lie beneath the surface. My hope is that this book can connect us in a way that opens the door to conversations and shared influence. Hopefully, you've been inspired to reflect and shine a light on your own unique story and path.

A hui hou kākou

Glossary of words and phrases used in the book

Auraii - just an expression - "Alright"

e hele kākou Hoʻomaka ʻia kēia huakai - Alright let's all start this adventure/journey.

ʻAe mai iaʻu Kela kaua - Let me fight for this

ʻāina - land, earth

A hui hou kākou - Until we meet again

haʻahaʻa - Its meaning is to be proud, by continuing well. Humility.

He hoʻailona paha - Maybe it's a sign, maybe it's meant to be.

He palena ʻole ka ʻike - unsurpassed knowledge.

hoʻomanaʻo - Remember.

hoʻomanaʻo mau - memento, souvenir, lasting remembrance

hoʻoponopono - to correct, to make right, also a ancient Hawaiian self-healing practice- also could be used to heal others.

I mua a lei i ka lei o ka lana kila - which means 'move forward and encircle yourself with the lei of victory

Ke aloha nui iā 'oukau pākahi a pau! - So much love for each and every one of you.

kuleana - responsibility, also right, privilege, concern,

Mahalo e ke akua - Thank god, thank you god.

Mahalo e ke akua no keia lā - Thank you lord for this day.

Mālama - to take care of the land

mana - the Hawaiian term meaning energy, power, or to have influence and the power to perform in a given situation

Manaiakalani - to be drawn in to something

mana'o - knowledge or deep knowledge

Mea ho'omana'o - souvenir, keepsake, reminder, memorandum

palena 'ole - vs. Boundless, without limit, vast.

Pono - can mean uprightness, excellence, in perfect order, and more according to the Hawaiian dictionary. If you are living pono, you are in right relationship with all people, places, and things in your life.

pule - prayer